finboroughtheatre

C000263983

JQ Productions in association with Neil McPherson for the Finborough Theatre presents

Death of Long Pig
by Nigel Planer

First performance at the Finborough Theatre, London:
Tuesday, 7 July 2009

Author's Note

Both Robert Louis Stevenson and Paul Gauguin went to live on South Pacific islands in the 1890s and died there within a few years of each other. They never met.

Whereas Stevenson, the eternal optimist, took with him to Samoa his widowed mother, his older wife, his stepchildren and stepgrandchild—the narcissistic and depressive Gauguin went alone to Tahiti and 'married' several young Tahitian and Marquesan girls, spawning children and descendants who are still around today.

Funded by royalties from *Dr Jekyll and Mr Hyde* and travel-writing commissions, the Stevensons had been able to voyage around the Pacific for four years before buying land in Samoa and building on it. They needed ongoing cash to subsidise their permanent emigration to a climate amenable to Stevenson's health.

To the end, Gauguin struggled to survive. Money from Paris from the rare sale of a painting was infrequent and he often resorted to writing subversive, caustic pieces for the local island newspapers, which led to his being ostracised by colonial society and, on one or two occasions, to his arrest.

The last decade of the nineteenth century was a turning point, culturally and politically, for the people of the South Seas. Their customs and religious practices were soon to be all but eliminated. The sexual ceremonies of the Tahitian 'Arii'oi' caste, the tradition of 'mahu', or transsexual males, and the ritual of cannibalism were either eradicated by the Church or subsumed into missionary projects within a few years of the date of this play.

Although each had his own personal reasons for ending up on the other side of the world, once there, both Stevenson and Gauguin tried – with varying degrees of success – first to understand the culture of the people they had arrived amongst, and later to represent and defend them from the oncoming colonial devastation.

"...the gods made with hands shall perish...Their glory, look! it is a bird's feathers, soon rotten; but our God is the same forever."
From *A Narrative of Missionary Enterprises in the South Sea Islands* by John Williams, of the London Missionary Society, who was clubbed to death and eaten on the beach at Eromanga in 1839.

Nigel Planer

Death of Long Pig
by **Nigel Planer**

Cast in order of appearance

Act One
Samoa, 1894

Louis	**Sean Murray**
Obliging Bob	**Anthony Ofoegbu**
Java	**Nicole Dayes**
Fanny	**Amanda Boxer**
Joe Strong	**Colm Gormley**

Act Two
Tahiti, 1897

Pigo	**Sean Murray**
Teha'amana	**Nicole Dayes**
Ben	**Colm Gormley**
Tiko	**Anthony Ofoegbu**
Othermother	**Amanda Boxer**

There will be one interval of fifteen minutes

The performance runs approximately 1 hour and 50 minutes

Directed by **Alexander Summers**
Designed by **Alex Marker**
Lighting Design by **James Smith**
Sound Design by **Andy Evans**
Costume Design by **Penn O'Gara**

Our patrons are respectfully reminded that, in this intimate theatre, any noise such as rustling programmes, talking or the ringing of mobile phones may distract the actors and your fellow audience members.

Interval drinks may be ordered in advance from the bar.

Amanda Boxer

Fanny Stevenson / Othermother

At the Finborough Theatre, Amanda has appeared in *The Destiny of Me* and *Many Roads to Paradise*.

Other theatre includes *The Last Days of Judas Iscariot* (Almeida Theatre), *The Pain and the Itch* (Royal Court Theatre), *No Shame, No Fear* (Jermyn Street Theatre), *Dis-Orientation* (Riverside Studios), *An Ideal Husband, The Rivals* (Clwyd Theatr Cymru), *One Last Card Trick* (Watford Palace Theatre), *Come Blow Your Horn, The Fall Guy, Absurd Person Singular* (Royal Exchange Theatre, Manchester), *The Arab Israeli Cookbook* (The Caird Company at the Tricycle Theatre), *Alice Virginia, Teresa* (New End Theatre), *A Small Family Business* (West Yorkshire Playhouse), *Angel* (The Shadow Factory), *Macbeth* (Arcola Theatre), *The Graduate* (Gielgud Theatre), *The Man Who Came to Dinner* (Chichester Festival Theatre), and *The Strip* (Royal Court Theatre).

Television includes *The Queen, Bodies 3, The Shell Seekers, Casualty, The Commander, Tom Brown's School Days, Trial And Retribution, Down To Earth, Chalk* (Series 2), *Road Rage, Goodbye My Love* and *Cider With Rosie*.

Film includes *Malice in Wonderland, Flight 93, Russian Dolls, Saving Private Ryan, Sorted* and *Bad Behaviour*.

Nicole Dayes

Java / Teha'amana

Trained at the Arts Educational Schools.

Productions whilst training included *The Love of the Nightingale, The Last Days of Judas Iscariot, Much Ado About Nothing, By the Beautiful Sea, Richard II, Betrayal, A Woman of No Importance, All My Sons, The Maids, Three Sisters and Someone Who'll Watch Over Me*.

Other theatre includes the rehearsed reading of *Estate Walls*, directed by Ché Walker (Theatre Royal, Stratford East).

Colm Gormley

Joe Strong / Ben

At the Finborough Theatre, Colm appeared in *The Ladies Cage* (also at the Royal Exchange Theatre, Manchester).

Other theatre includes *Twelfth Night* (York Theatre Royal), *The Boy with the Bomb in his Crisps* (Belgrade Theatre, Coventry), *All's Well That Ends Well, I'll Be the Devil* (Royal Shakespeare Company), *The Water Harvest, The Time Step* (Theatre 503), *Smilin' Through* (The Drill Hall), *We, The People* (Shakespeare's Globe), *Merry Christmas Betty Ford* (Lyric Theatre, Belfast), *The Early Bird* (national tour), *Elizabeth* (national tour), *The Blind Bird* (Gate Theatre), *The Resistible Rise of Arturo Ui, The White Devil, The Three Sisters, Romeo and Juliet, A Midsummer Night's Dream, The Seagull, Family Voices, The Europeans* and *The Bay at Nice* (Mercury Theatre, Colchester).

Television and film includes *The Message, Ultimate Force* and *Omagh*.

Sean Murray

Louis / Pigo

Theatre includes *The English Game* (Headlong), *The Home Place* (Comedy Theatre), *Buried Child* (National Theatre), *Jane Eyre* (Shared Experience), *The Crucible* (The Touring Consortium), *The Cherry Orchard, The Phoenician Women, The Virtuoso, The Two Gentlemen of Verona, Romeo and Juliet, A Woman Killed with Kindness, Amphibians* (Royal Shakespeare Company), *The Fairy Queen* (Aix-en-Provence Festival), *Othello, The Comedy of Errors, The Life of Galileo, The Rivals, Tartuffe, The School for Scandal, Judy, Androcles and the Lion, A Little Hotel on the Side* (Bristol Old Vic), *The Misanthrope* (Cambridge Theatre Company), *For King and Country* (Greenwich Theatre) and *One Flew Over the Cuckoo's Nest* (Redgrave Theatre, Farnham).

Television includes *Robin Hood, Casualty, Judge John Deed, Dunkirk, Holby City, Serious and Organised, Silent Witness, Without Motive, The Bill, A Wing and a Prayer, Berkeley Square, A Rather English Marriage, Peak Practice, Seaforth, Smokescreen, Advocates, The March, South of the Border, The Country Boy* and *EastEnders*.

Film includes *Hamlet, The Truth* and *Finding Mallory*.

Radio includes *Starlight's Apprentice, Saint Nick, The Chimes* and *The Pirates Are Coming*.

Anthony Ofoegbu

Obliging Bob / Tiko

Theatre includes *Death and the King's Horseman* (National Theatre), *This Child* (Theatre Royal York), *35 Cents* (Blue Elephant Theatre), *Twelfth Night* (Theatre Royal, Northampton), *The Lion and the Jewel* (The Pit, Barbican), *Topdog/Underdog* (Project Theatre, Dublin), *Hurl* (Tivoli Theatre, Dublin), *King Baabu* (Baxter Theatre, Cape Town, and International Tour), *Long Time No See* (Talawa Theatre), *The Meeting* (Jepsom Theatre, University of Richmond), *Oedipus at Colonus* (Nevada Conservatory Theatre and Delphi), *The Blond* (Cockpit Theatre), *The Twits* (Belgrade Theatre, Coventry), *Treemonisha* (Hackney Empire), *Ondine* (Cochrane Theatre), *The Beatification Of Area Boy* (West Yorkshire Playhouse and International Tour), and *Once On This Island* (Royalty Theatre).

Television includes *Spooks, Casualty, Chambers, Family Affairs* and *The Bill*.

Film includes *Bad Day, Dead Room, Plato's Breaking Point, The Killing Zone* and *Samson and Delilah*.

Radio includes BBC Radio 4 repertory company.

Nigel Planer Playwright

After studying African and Asian Studies at Sussex University and training as an actor at LAMDA, Nigel became a co-founder of London's Comedy Store and Comic Strip clubs and went on to star in the TV classics *The Young Ones* and *The Comic Strip Presents*. His first play, *On the Ceiling* opened at the Birmingham Repertory Theatre and transferred to the Garrick Theatre. More recently, it was revived at the Landor Theatre in London and was a Saturday play on BBC Radio 4. Although best known for comedy, Nigel Planer has appeared in many drama series and films, and in new plays at the Young Vic, Bush Theatre, West Yorkshire Playhouse, Traverse Theatre, Edinburgh, and Hampstead Theatre. He has co-written episodes of *King and Castle* (with Andy de la Tour) and *Funseekers* (with Doug Lucie). He has also written two critically acclaimed novels – *The Right Man*, and *Faking It* – the best-selling *A Good Enough Dad*, and the spoof theatrical biography *I, An Actor* (with Christopher Douglas). He has published a short collection of poetry – *Unlike the Buddha*, and regularly contributed to *The Guardian* poetry spot in the 1990s.

Alexander Summers Director

At the Finborough Theatre, Alexander was Resident Assistant Director during 2007 where he directed *A Letter to England*, a double bill including the first play by Pearson Award Bursary winner Anders Lustgarten, and was Assistant Director on Nicholas de Jongh's *Plague Over England*, the *Time Out* Critics' Choice production of *Ours, Lucifer Saved, Men Without Shadows, The Lower Depths, The Ladies Cage* and *Love Child*. Trained at Manchester University and with Cheek by Jowl. Other directing includes *Myth, Propaganda and Disaster* (Contact Theatre, Manchester), *Much Ado About Nothing* and *The Man with the Flower in His Mouth* (both at the Bridewell Theatre), *Troubleshooters* (Soho Theatre), *Coriolanus* (Brockley Jack Theatre), *For the Public Good* (Baron's Court Theatre), *The Lover* (John Thaw Studio, Manchester), *Glengarry Glen Ross* (Manchester Fringe Festival Award Winner). He led artistic programming for the Czech theatre retrospective *A Cautious Path* (Tristan Bates Theatre), and was Assistant Director on *Uncertainty* (Latitude Festival). He is also currently Apprentice Director on the Theatre Royal Haymarket's production of *Waiting for Godot*.

Alex Marker Designer

At the Finborough Theatre, Alex is Resident Designer where he has designed twenty productions including *Charlie's Wake, The Women's War, How I Got That Story, Soldiers, Happy Family, Trelawny of the 'Wells', Hortensia and the Museum of Dreams, Albert's Boy, Lark Rise to Candleford, Red Night, The Representative, Love Child, Eden's Empire, Little Madam, Plague Over England* (and the subsequent West End transfer to the Duchess Theatre), *Hangover Square, Sons Of York, Untitled*, and *Painting a Wall*, as well as Associate Designer on *Blackwater Angel*. Other designs include *The Real McCoy Reconnected* (Hackney Empire), *The Viewing Room* (Arts Theatre), *School's Theatre Festival* (Young Vic), *Origin: Unknown* (Theatre Royal, Stratford East), *My Real War 1914 – ?* (National Tour), *Sweet Charity* (Theatre Royal, Drury Lane), *The Pink Bedroom* (Courtyard Theatre), *Cherry Docs* (King's Head Theatre), *An Eligible Man* (New End Theatre), *King Arthur* (Arcola Theatre), *Hush* (Arcola Theatre and Pleasance Edinburgh), *Cooking With Elvis* (Lyceum Theatre, Crewe) and *Oklahoma!* (New Wimbledon Theatre). His work has been exhibited several times, most recently in *Collaborators: UK Design for Performance* exhibition in Nottingham. www.alexmarker.com

Penn O'Gara Costume Designer

At the Finborough Theatre, Penn was Costume Designer on *Lullabies of Broadmoor*, *Masks and Faces*, *Lark Rise to Candleford*, *Trelawny of the 'Wells'*, *Plague Over England*, *Hangover Square* and *Country Magic*. She has a Master of Fine Arts degree in Costume Design from Southern Methodist University, Dallas Other designs include *Roman Nights* and *Pete'n'Me* (New End Theatre), *The Shadow Box* (Southwark Playhouse), *Diary of a Madman* (Rondo Theatre, Bath), *Far Away*, *Shang-a-Lang* and *Two Noble Kinsmen* (Bristol Old Vic), *Antigone* (Ustinov Studio, Bath), *Seven Go Mad in Thebes*, *The Crucible*, *The Magic Flute* and *The Barber of Seville* (QEH, Bristol), *A Kind of Alaska*, *Stairway to Heaven*, *Macbeth*, *Deathsong* and *Derby Day* (Alma Theatre, Bristol), and *Aida*, *Macbeth*, *Die Fledermaus* and *Nabucco* (Victoria Rooms, Bristol).

James Smith Lighting Designer

At the Finborough theatre, James was Lighting Designer for *Eyes Catch Fire*, *Ordinary Days*, *Untitled* and *Painting A Wall*. Recent theatre as lighting designer includes *The Extra Factor* (national tour), *Cinderella* (Hackney Empire), *Sweet Charity* (Stratford Circus), *One Flew Over the Cuckoo's Nest* (BAC) and *Picture Perfect* (national tour). James works as an Associate Lighting Designer to both Mark Jonathan and Howard Harrison and has worked on *The Music Man* (Chichester Festival Theatre), *Jane Eyre* (London Children's Ballet) and *The Circle* (Chichester Festival Theatre and national tour). Other selected projects as Assistant Lighting Designer include *Babes in Arms* (Chichester Festival Theatre), *Macbeth* (Chichester Festival Theatre and Gielgud Theatre), *The Wizard of Oz* (Birmingham Rep), *Nicholas Nickleby* (Chichester Festival Theatre, national tour, London and Toronto), *Skellig* (Young Vic), and *Suddenly Last Summer* (Crucible Theatre, Sheffield and national tour). Relights include *Tracy Beaker – Get Real* (national tour) and *London Assurance* (Watermill Theatre, Newbury, and national tour). James also works as a freelance lecturer in Lighting Design and Lighting Management at Rose Bruford College.

Andy Evans Sound Designer

Trained at RADA.
Productions designed whilst training included *Dolly Wests Kitchen*, *Man Equals Man*, *The Madras House and Boxergirl*. Recent theatre as sound designer includes *Boticelli's Bonfire* (national welsh tour*), Little Mermaid the musical* (Barry Memorial Theatre), *The Miniaturists* (Arcola Theatre), *On the Brink* (Circus Space London) and *My Favourite Year* (Bridewell Theatre). As a Sound Engineer and operator credits include *Festa* , *King lear*, *Pictures from an exhibition* and *Kursk* (Young Vic theatre). Other work includes Sound number 1 for *Horrid Henry* (Trafalgar studios) and *Macbeth* (Theatre Clwyd Cymru).

Ellie Browning Assistant Director

At the Finborough Theatre, Ellie is a Resident Assistant Director where she has assisted on *Untitled* and *The Killing of Mr Toad*, and has also stage managed *Oohrah!*, *Sons of York* and *Many Roads to Paradise*. Trained at Middlesex University. Other Assistant Directing includes *Who Will Carry the Word?* (Courtyard Theatre).

James Quaife Producer

Founded by James Quaife in 2008, JQ Productions is committed to producing high-quality theatre in the UK and is dedicated to the producing and staging of ambitious productions. Previous productions include *Painting a Wall* by David Lan (Finborough Theatre), *Orpheus* by Kenneth McLeish (BAC) and *Vigil*, based on the poetry of Maurice Maeterlinck (Tristan Bates Theatre). Forthcoming productions include the European premiere of the musical *Little Fish* by Michael John LaChiusa at the Finborough Theatre in November 2009. www.jamesquaife.com

finboroughtheatre

"One of the most stimulating venues in London, fielding a programme that is a bold mix of trenchant, politically thought-provoking new drama and shrewdly chosen revivals of neglected works from the past." *The Independent*

"A disproportionately valuable component of the London theatre ecology. Its programme combines new writing and revivals, in selections intelligent and audacious." *Financial Times*

"A blazing beacon of intelligent endeavour, nurturing new writers while finding and reviving neglected curiosities from home and abroad." *The Daily Telegraph*

"Few leading fringe theatres have walked off with so many awards or promoted such a rich variety of writers as the Finborough." *Plays International*

"The Finborough Theatre has developed a reputation out of all proportion to its tiny size. It has played its part in the careers of many remarkable playwrights, directors, and actors." *Financial Times*

The multi-award-winning Finborough Theatre – led by Artistic Director Neil McPherson – presents both plays and music theatre, concentrated exclusively on new writing and rediscoveries of neglected works from the 19th and 20th centuries. We also run a Resident Assistant Director Programme and a vibrant Literary Department.

Founded in 1980, artists working at the theatre in the 1980's included Clive Barker, Rory Bremner, Nica Burns, Kathy Burke, Ken Campbell and Clare Dowie. In the 1990's, the Finborough Theatre became particularly known for new writing including Naomi Wallace's first play *The War Boys*; Rachel Weisz in David Farr's *Neville Southall's Washbag*; four plays by Anthony Neilson including *Penetrator* and *The Censor*, both of which transferred to the Royal Court Theatre; and new plays by Tony Marchant, David Eldridge, Mark Ravenhill and Phil Willmott. New writing development included Mark Ravenhill's *Shopping and F***king* (Royal Court, West End and Broadway), Conor McPherson's *This Lime Tree Bower* (Bush Theatre) and Naomi Wallace's *Slaughter City* (Royal Shakespeare Company).

Since 2000, New British plays have included Laura Wade's London debut with her adaptation of W.H. Davies' *Young Emma*, commissioned for the Finborough Theatre; Simon Vinnicombe's *Year 10* which went on to play at BAC's Time Out Critics' Choice Season; James Graham's *Albert's Boy* with Victor Spinetti; Joy Wilkinson's *Fair* which transferred to the West End; and Nicholas de Jongh's *Plague Over England*, which transferred to the West End. London premieres have included Jack Thorne's *Fanny and Faggot* which also transferred to the West End. Many of the Finborough Theatre's new plays have been published and are on sale from our website.

UK premieres of foreign plays have included Brad Fraser's *Wolfboy*; Lanford Wilson's *Sympathetic Magic*; Larry Kramer's *The Destiny of Me*; Tennessee Williams' *Something Cloudy, Something Clear*; Frank McGuinness' *Gates of Gold* with William Gaunt and the late John Bennett in his last stage role (which also transferred to the West End); *Nilo Cruz's Hortensia and the Museum of Dreams* with Linda Bassett; the English premiere of Robert McLellan's Scots language classic, *Jamie the Saxt*; and Joe DiPietro's *F***king Men*, currently playing at the King's Head Theatre.

Rediscoveries of neglected work have included the first London revivals of Rolf Hochhuth's *Soldiers and The Representative*; both parts of Keith Dewhurst's *Lark Rise to Candleford*; The *Women's War*, an evening of original suffragette plays; *Etta Jenks* with Clarke Peters and Daniela Nardini; *The Gigli Concert* with Niall Buggy and Paul McGann; Noël Coward's first play,

The Rat Trap; Charles Wood's *Jingo* with Susannah Harker; and the sell-out production of Patrick Hamilton's *Hangover Square*.

Music Theatre has included the new (premieres from the UK and USA by Grant Olding, Charles Miller, Michael John LaChuisa, Adam Guettel, Andrew Lippa and Adam Gwon) and the old (the sell-out Celebrating British Music Theatre series, reviving forgotten British musicals).

The Finborough Theatre was the inaugural winner of the Empty Space Peter Brook Award's Dan Crawford Pub Theatre Award in 2005 which it also won again in 2008, as well as winning the Empty Space Peter Brook Mark Marvin Award in 2004. The Finborough Theatre was the only unfunded theatre to be awarded the prestigious Pearson Playwriting Award bursary for Chris Lee in 2000, Laura Wade in 2005, James Graham in 2006, Al Smith in 2007 and Anders Lustgarten in 2009 – as well as the Pearson Award for Best Play for Laura Wade in 2005 and James Graham in 2007. Neil McPherson was named Best Artistic Director in the 2009 Fringe Report Awards.

www.finboroughtheatre.co.uk

finboroughtheatre
118 Finborough Road, London SW10 9ED
admin@finboroughtheatre.co.uk
www.finboroughtheatre.co.uk

Artistic Director | **Neil McPherson**
Resident Designer | **Alex Marker**
General Manager | **Anna Bartholomew**
Pearson Playwright-in-Residence | **Anders Lustgarten**
Playwrights-in-Residence | **James Graham, Al Smith, Alexandra Wood**
Literary Associate | **Titas Halder**
Production Coordinator | **Ben Cooper**
Resident Casting Director | **Rachel Payant**
Chief Electrician | **Oliver Luff**
Master Carpenter | **Jessi James**
Resident Assistant Directors | **Ellie Browning, Tim Newns, Eleanor Rhode**

Mailing
Join our free mailing list. Give your details to our Box Office staff or email admin@finboroughtheatre.co.uk.

Feedback
We welcome your comments, complaints and suggestions. Write to Finborough Theatre, 118 Finborough Road, London SW10 9ED or email the Artistic Director at neilmcpherson@finboroughtheatre.co.uk

Friends
The Finborough Theatre is a registered charity. We receive no public funding, and rely solely on the support of our audiences. Please do consider supporting us by becoming a member of our Friends of the Finborough Theatre scheme. There are four categories of Friends, each offering a wide range of benefits.
Richard Tauber Friends – Charles Lascelles.
Lionel Monckton Friends – Anonymous. Philip and Christine Carne.
William Terriss Friends – Tom Erhardt. Leo and Janet Liebster. Peter Lobl.

Smoking is not permitted in the auditorium and the use of cameras and recording equipment is strictly prohibited.

In accordance with the requirements of the Royal Borough of Kensington and Chelsea:
1. The public may leave at the end of the performance by all doors and such doors must at that time be kept open.
2. All gangways, corridors, staircases and external passageways intended for exit shall be left entirely free from obstruction whether permanent or temporary.
3. Persons shall not be permitted to stand or sit in any of
the gangways intercepting the seating or to sit in any of the other gangways.

The Finborough Theatre has the support of the Pearson Playwrights' Scheme. Sponsored by Pearson PLC.

The Finborough Theatre is a member of the Independent Theatre Council and Musical Theatre Matters UK

The Finborough Theatre is licensed by the Royal Borough of Kensington and Chelsea to The Steam Industry, a registered charity and a company limited by guarantee. Registered in England no. 3448268. Registered Charity no. 1071304. Registered Office: 118 Finborough Road, London SW10 9ED. The Steam Industry is under the Artistic Direction of Phil Willmott. www.philwillmott.co.uk

Death of Long Pig
Production Acknowledgements
Stage Manager | **Sophie Wynter**
Assistant Stage Manager | **Katy Mills**
Casting Consultant | **Rachel Payant**
Casting and Production Assistant | **Jennifer Littlewood**
Scenic Painting Assistant | **Eleanor Collins**
Design Assistant | **Joanna Ebling**
Website and Graphic Design | **Liam Bowers for LAB Experiments**
Illustration | **Chris Rixon**
Film Trailer | **Damien Pollard www.damienpollard.com**
Production Photography | **Stuart Allen www.stuartallenphotos.com**
Cultural Workshop Leaders | **Tahiarii and Rosanna Raymond**
Marketing and Publicity | **Stefanie Wardow**
Production Administration | **Lawrence Summers**
Lighting Hire | **Stage Electrics**
Press Representative | **Neil McPherson** admin@finboroughtheatre.co.uk
Production rehearsed at the Jerwood Space with thanks to Richard Lee

With support from
Graham Benson and Christen Benson on behalf of Blue Heaven Productions Ltd, Jamie Rix on behalf of Little Brother Productions, David Green and Judy Green, Rosemary Ann Sisson, Peter Rosengard and Keir Prince.

With special thanks to
Sir Ian McKellen, Nick Hern, Emma Deakin, Blanche Marvin, Dominic Rowan, Paola Dionisotti, Jeffery Kissoon, Chloe Thomas, David Schofield, John Warnaby, Rebecca Peyton, Scott Ainslie, Dr Jenny Newell, Francesca Rowan, Roberta Green, Roger Quaife, Philip Currie, Elanor Collins, Hilary Strong, Linda Dryden, Claudia Sermbezis, David and Jane Fanshawe and The Questors Theatre.

In loving memory of Jamie Thomson

DEATH OF LONG PIG

Nigel Planer

Characters

ACT ONE	ACT TWO
LOUIS *Robert Louis Stevenson*	**PIGO** *Paul Gauguin*
FANNY *his wife*	**OTHERMOTHER** *his mother-in-law*
JOE *Joe Strong, their son-in-law*	**BEN** *the storekeeper*
OBLIGING BOB *the groundsman*	**TIKO** *a neighbour*
JAVA *the maid*	**TEHA'AMANA** *Pigo's 'wife'*

Settings

Samoa, 1894   Tahiti, 1897

The play is written for five actors who double characters in the two acts as indicated above.

This text went to press before the end of rehearsals and so may differ slightly from the play as performed.

ACT ONE

Otherworldly music; Polynesian women singing a mournful hymn and chanting. Lights up on LOUIS *lying 'in state', draped in a Union Jack that has been almost covered by Polynesian fabrics ('tapas') draped over it. Flowers all around.* LOUIS *lies with his elbows over the drapes, hands clasped on his chest, eyes closed, cheeks hollow.*

Two Samoan islanders stand or sit nearby. They are in various states of mourning. They are staff from LOUIS' *home;* OBLIGING BOB *and* JAVA. JAVA *is crying.* OBLIGING BOB *comes forward, solemnly. The hymn singing and chanting dies down enough for him to speak, but remains subliminally.* OBLIGING BOB *intones a funeral oration.*

OBLIGING BOB.
>'This be the verse you grave for me...
>This is where he longed to be...
>Home is the sailor home from the sea...
>And the hunter home from the hill.
>Under the wide and starry sky...
>Dig the grave and let me lie...
>Glad did I live and gladly die...

He is overcome with emotion and has to rally himself to say the last line.

>And... And I lay me down... with... I lay me down with...

LOUIS (*from the bed*). With a will. 'I lay me down with a will.'

OBLIGING BOB.
>And I lay me down with a will.'

>There.

LOUIS sits upright suddenly, irritated.

LOUIS. Where's Fanny? She should be here. She should be standing there next to you, Java, to be precise.

JAVA. Mrs Stevenson is in her room, Mr RLS. She no come out for three days.

LOUIS. Oh dear. Not again. Ohh. Did you call her?

JAVA. She stop eating again, Mr RLS.

LOUIS. Oh no. Did you tell her how important it is she join us?

OBLIGING BOB. If you don't mind me saying, old boy, I think Mrs Stevenson finds such rehearsals enervating and hard to take.

LOUIS. I know that, Bob, old chap, and she is wrong. A bit of practice will help her to be less agitated on the day. We are planning quite a gala.

He jumps up and starts to pace up and down, agitatedly.

OBLIGING BOB. That's it. She might find it easier on the nerves if you were intending to pass on quietly, without the hoo-haa, from some unmarked hut.

LOUIS. No. One must die contiguously, with one's family around one – as many as one can reasonably muster – a wife, and children too preferably, and if there are none of those, then someone else's will have to do.

OBLIGING BOB. Yes. Lloyd and Belle send their apologies and assurances that they will be there on the day, for bang certain. But it was felt that little Austin was perhaps too young…

LOUIS. Too many childish questions for them all to answer, no doubt. About the nature of mortality.

LOUIS *coughs. The others look to see how serious it is.*

I need their permission, you see, Bob. Before I can shuffle off to the other side. I will need all of their permission to go.

JAVA *starts to cry again.*

My dear Java, that's exactly right. Well done. At least someone is taking this seriously.

OBLIGING BOB. The silly girl's afraid your ghost will get lost in transit on the way to Edinburgh, but you belong to us now. I have explained that to her.

LOUIS. Quite right. My spirit, if I have one, will be staying right here, Java, for the duration.

JAVA. But I think there's a bad one Tiapolo gonna get you then.

LOUIS (*laughing*). Have no fear, Java, dear thing, your island spirits of the dead will have no interest in preying on a Scotsman. The Tupapa'o [*pronounced 'Tooper-pow'*] won't come here. One bite o' me and they'd have a thistle in their craw.

LOUIS laughs at his own joke which induces a fit of coughing. He collapses onto the bed to cough.

OBLIGING BOB (*intoning the verse again, over* LOUIS' *cough*).
'This be the verse you grave for me...
This is where he longed to be...
Home is the sailor home from the sea...
And the hunter home from the hill...'

While OBLIGING BOB *recites,* JAVA *takes a tapa cloth and starts to cover* LOUIS *with it.* LOUIS, *still coughing, tries, weakly, to resist.*

LOUIS (*through coughing*). Java! Bob! It's not time! Java! I'm not a kanaka! Not an islander! Bob!

But OBLIGING BOB *continues to repeat the verses and* JAVA *covers* LOUIS *up completely so that he cannot be seen.*

The underscored chanting has given way to aggressive Maori drumming, which blends with the sounds of LOUIS' *coughing, which has been amplified.*

Samoa, 1894.

The stage space now represents the main downstairs room at Vailima, the home of Robert Louis Stevenson and his family and staff. A large, airy room with a wooden floor.

Sunshine is coming in from a doorway which leads out to a spacious verandah and lawns beyond. In the corner, at an angle, is a very large metal safe which looks rather like a Smeg fridge – it is over six foot tall. There might also be double doors to where the front verandah would be, with steps down to the front lawn. The room has a feeling of light and space. Light is coming from windows on all sides except the side where the rest of the house is.

The flowers are gone. But there is perhaps a hint of the jungle intruding into this house. Perhaps a tree is growing through a corner, perhaps there are hidden bamboo masks in the shadows.

It is a beautiful morning.

Long pause, then...

LOUIS (*offstage*). I think I may be well enough to come downstairs unassisted!

Pause.

I am coming down the stairs. Fanny...? Here I come!

Slowly from the top of the 'stairs', LOUIS enters, hanging onto a bannister, if there is one. He is wearing white sultan trousers, Cossack boots, a white kaftan shirt with a coloured sash and a large cloak. He gets halfway and stops for breath.

LOUIS *is forty-four years old, tanned and bony. He has a large zapata moustache and lively, intelligent eyes. He is a very charismatic man.*

I am coming downstairs unassisted!

He looks around the room. There is no one around.

Fanny?!

He gives up and starts up the 'stairs' again. He exits. Pause. FANNY comes running on, in a flap. She is covered in earth from doing the gardening.

FANNY *is ten years older than* LOUIS, *but no less eccentric. She is wearing a voluminous, blue 'Mother Hubbard', or missionary smock with lacework around the neck and shoulders. Physically she is the opposite of* LOUIS, *sturdy and big-boned where he is angular. She is an Anglo-Creole American. She is stressed and neurotic.*

FANNY. Louis? Louis? Everybody?! Louis is coming downstairs on his own! Belle? Lloyd? Louis is getting up!

She checks her appearance in the mirror, then goes to the double doors and shouts to the servants outside.

Are you there, Louis? Bob! Quickly! Louis is getting up! Come quickly to congratulate him! Java! Java! (*She tuts that* JAVA *is not there.*)

Pause.

FANNY *waits at the bottom of the 'stairs'.* LOUIS *makes a sweeping entrance.* FANNY *gasps.*

LOUIS. I – am – vertical! And what is more, locomotive! Slight dizziness, some nausea, but gastric and biliary with congestion, not catarrhal. (*He feels his neck.*) Pulse-rate somewhat up, a small amount of sweat but the spirits of the dead, with whom we share our island home, have fled! My fever has subsided!

He descends quite quickly to the landing.

FANNY. Java! The Tusitala is up! Louis, are you quite sure?

LOUIS. The demonic Tupapa'o must return to their netherworld, and wait a little longer for me to join their dark chorus! I dreamed I was dead, my darling.

FANNY. And have you taken any of your mixture today?

LOUIS. Sometimes it is hard to tell whether it is the fever itself, or your medications cause these visions in the night.

JAVA enters, running. She is overjoyed to see LOUIS *up. She starts to help when she sees him, but he waves her back.*

JAVA is a teenage islander from a village about a mile away. She is very hard-working and reliable. She is wearing a muted brown tapa, or Samoan wrap-around sarong.

FANNY. Java, it's all right, I can manage quite well enough on my own now.

LOUIS. Ah! Java, Java! The 'mana' has returned. My life force is back! I am strong! In fact, I feel as if I had just cannibalistically devoured a hundred of your dead ancestors, Java, and now possess their 'mana' as well as my own…! Although I may need assistance to get me to the verandah. Ooof! Where is Bob?

FANNY (*calling through door into garden*). Bob! Bob! Better get in here now! Louis is walking most precariously. Java? Where is Belle?

JAVA. She gone to Apia, ma'am, with Lloyd.

LOUIS. Oh, is the ship in? What have they gone to buy?

FANNY (*looking accusingly at* JAVA). Oil, Louis. We ran out of oil again.

JAVA *looks at the floor.*

Oh, Lloyd will be so sad he missed your revival. He would love to get a photograph of you walking again for his journals. Lloyd's gone to town, Louis, can't you wait to get up until he gets back?

LOUIS. Certainly not! He can take me as I am when he arrives!

During the following, FANNY *helps* LOUIS *towards a table. She takes almost too much care.* JAVA *arranges a place at the table and prepares a chair with cushions.* FANNY *shoos her out of the way. When they get to the table,* LOUIS *does not sit down, but stands, clinging onto the edge of it.*

I should hate to spoil this moment of rebirth with a tawdry thought, but I have to ask, Java, why you are not correctly dressed?

JAVA. Madam…

LOUIS. What?

JAVA. …Mrs Stevenson… said… when you were ill… no need…

LOUIS. No need to dress for dinner??

JAVA. Please, Mr RLS, it is only just now breakfast is finished.

LOUIS. Is it?

FANNY. Louis my dear, it is not yet nine. Maybe you are still a trifle delirious? Might you perhaps be able to eat something? Some breakfast in bed?

JAVA. Mr RLS hungry now?

LOUIS. Yes, yes. I am ravenous. I could eat a high priest or two.

JAVA. Mrs Stevenson? Should I bring Mr RLS some banana pudding now?

LOUIS. Oooh, yes please!

FANNY. Well...

JAVA. And coffee?

LOUIS. Do we have coffee? Splendid! Thank you so much, m'dear!

FANNY. Coffee, Louis? I think not.

JAVA *starts to go.*

LOUIS. Oh, and Java?

JAVA (*turning*). Yes?

LOUIS. Teine merahi noa noa [*pronounced 'Tay-eenay mer-arnee noa noa'*]. (*Then, to* FANNY.) Doesn't Java smell nice?

JAVA (*smiling*). Tch tch!

JAVA *exits.*

LOUIS. Did we not decide to dress for all meals? Wasn't that it?

FANNY. No, my darling, just dinner. But it is so wonderful to have you up. I will go and change. If you can wait. But will you be all right to sit alone for so many minutes, so soon after getting up? Perhaps you will get dizzy! What a dilemma!

LOUIS. No, no. If you can tolerate a man so over-kitted-out for a mere breakfast, then I shall make my way directly to the verandah to eat.

FANNY (*crossly*). Well, I offered...

LOUIS. But what of you? How have you been? Have you heard from your voices again?

FANNY. I don't know what you're talking about.

LOUIS. Any recurrence? Or is all quiet now? Do you have still-ness of mind?

FANNY. I am not insane, Louis! As all your friends would have it!

LOUIS. No. But you cannot put us all through that again, Fanny.

FANNY. Yes, it is so heartening to hear you have an appetite. And since you are so determined to enter the bustle of the day, is it possible you might even start writing again? Belle will be happy to be occupied once more! She has been quite wilted with nothing to do since you have been in bed.

LOUIS. Bed? My darling, I have been back down to the very banks of the dark river and stared into that void where the Other Fellow dwells!

FANNY. Yes, but now you have returned to us, and normality. And...

LOUIS. And as I climbed back up, unlike Orpheus, I did not look back, for fear I would have found myself looking at my own reflection! I will dictate to Belle as soon as she returns from her spending spree.

OBLIGING BOB *enters through the door from the garden. He is carrying flowers and big bunches of greenery.*

OBLIGING BOB *is from one of the nearby islands. He might have a tattoo on his face. He is wearing a Scottish tartan tapa/sarong and perhaps has a flower over his ear.*

OBLIGING BOB. So good! So good! Three hurrahs for the Laird of Vailima!

LOUIS. Good day to you, Bob!

> 'An' Louis' deid. The mair's the pity!
> He's deid, an' deid o'Aquae-vitae.
> O Embro', you're a shrunken city,
> Noo puer Louis' deid!

OBLIGING BOB (*joining in*).
> To see him was baith drink an' meat,
> Gaun linkin' glegly up the street!'

LOUIS. Good to see you, Bob, and how it cheers me to see you wearing that tartan lavalava! How is the road to my tomb?

During the following, OBLIGING BOB *puts the flowers and greenery in various places around the room.* FANNY *rearranges them neatly after him.*

OBLIGING BOB. Oh boy! It's as swell and gummy as can be! You can come and see for yourself what we have cleared so far, if you like.

FANNY. No. Thank you, Bob. Perhaps in a day or two when Louis has recovered sufficiently.

LOUIS. So, not finished? Maybe I could take a look at the work in progress? Just from the verandah?

FANNY *tuts.*

Some sunshine might restore my smashed-up constitution after I have eaten. Bob, would you care to join me for breakfast?

FANNY *tuts.*

OBLIGING BOB (*aware of* FANNY*'s disapproval*). Thank you heartily, but no. It shall endure for ever, the road that we are building to your grave!

LOUIS. You and the lads will be relieved at my temporary recovery today. It has given you an extended contract to finish the work.

OBLIGING BOB. Nonsense, old man! We'll be done in no time! Every damned chap on the island wants to lend a hand! And all of the fellows from the old Calaboose Prison! They all want to show their gratitude! You can pass on any time you like!

FANNY. Bob! You make it sound as if you positively desire it!

OBLIGING BOB. Mrs Stevenson. With respect, when the time comes I will be as jolly well heart-stricken and wretched as the next man – the very stones and earth will weep with me – but now I just want the great man to know that things will go tickety-boo on the day.

LOUIS. Ala Loto Alofa [*'Road of the Loving Heart' in Samoan*]!! Ah, my Road of the Loving Hearts! I will go gladly on that final path.

OBLIGING BOB. Your road to paradise shall never be muddy! And as we climb it, carrying you aloft, sweet-smelling limes will edge us on each side, right to the very top of Mount Vaea!

FANNY. Bob, please. To talk of Louis' funeral arrangements so early in the morning is not appropriate, I think.

OBLIGING BOB. It was your blessed husband who sprung those lads from the cursed Calaboose with his negotiation and persuading of the authorities. We would be less than men to deny him the sending-off of his choice.

LOUIS. And ten muskets resound for my salute! Or at any rate, old Fala E'ianao [*pronounced 'Ee-ar-now'*] on the bongo drum.

OBLIGING BOB. And everyone will sing. And everyone will have a cake.

FANNY. Louis. Must we? Please?

LOUIS. My darling Western wife, to an islander his grave is what our clocks are to us. Always keeping time. Old Tapiteu [*pronounced 'Tappy-tayoo'*], when he fell badly ill with a fever, went out, dug a grave for himself by the roadside and stood in it and stayed there for a fortnight, eating, smoking with passers-by, which made him feel much better. So he packed up and went home.

OBLIGING BOB. With respect, Mrs Stevenson, in these parts, the mere sight of a coffin has been known to shake off the hand of death.

FANNY. But you are no islander, Louis. We have an entire pharmacy upstairs.

LOUIS. Fanny, I have spent thirty years in rigorous combat with the Reaper. When he finally wins, as win he must, I will not slink away from his victory parade, but claim it as my own, with guns and flags and solemn songs and an absolute killer march for everyone else, right up the side of the mountain to the very top on my beautiful road!

FANNY. But so wretched to be thinking of that now, my sweet. Might not your freely breathing hours be better spent in composition?

LOUIS. I do believe, my dear, that you are envious. Jealous of my mountaintop memorial plaque. Have no fear, I have written a verse for you as well, to come and lie beside me when you croak.

OBLIGING BOB (*intoning the verse*).
    'A fellow traveller, true through life...

LOUIS (*trying to stop him*). Erm, thank you, Bob...

OBLIGING BOB.
    Teacher, tender comrade, wife!'

FANNY. 'Comrade'?!

LOUIS. Perhaps it does need a bit of work.

FANNY. The only way you'll get me to go up that mountain is after I am gone – in a jar.

LOUIS. Where's little Austin?

FANNY. He must have gone into Apia with Belle. We should have a photograph of you with little Austin.

LOUIS. I wish I were eight years old again. How I love that little boy! (*To* OBLIGING BOB.) Dear Obliging Bob, I wonder if you could be so good as to hold my robe, it is rather heavy. Don't go too far with it. I may need to put it on again should Lloyd return and want to take a photograph.

OBLIGING BOB *obliges, and hangs the cloak over a chair.* LOUIS *tries a couple of poses in the mirror as if for a photograph. But he is stiff from lying down for some days.*

(*As he disrobes.*) It is how we prepare for our own deaths, that determines how well we live our lives. Or was it the other way round?

FANNY. Louis! Stop it!

LOUIS. I fear that is all the energy I have today. I must sit down and eat if I am to perambulate on the verandah.

He sits ceremoniously at the table, with help from FANNY *and* OBLIGING BOB. *All three are aware of the care that must be taken.* LOUIS *breathes deeply and smiles. He coughs.*

Both FANNY *and* OBLIGING BOB *freeze for a moment to see if the cough will develop. It doesn't.* LOUIS *relaxes again.*

There! Now, where's my banana pudding?

JOE STRONG *enters.* JOE *is in his early thirties, American, tanned. He is* FANNY's *son-in-law. A shifty-looking fellow wearing an odd mix of Samoan and Western clothes. His tapa/sarong is flower-patterned and flamboyant and his hair is wild. There is something of the sulky teenager about him.*

JOE. Hello, Louis.

LOUIS. Good day to you, Joe, my Tiapolo, my darker side. How are things in the underworld? You devil, you! You chinch!

OBLIGING BOB.
     'I am the smiler with the knife,
     In solemn sanctimonious state…

LOUIS (*to* JOE). As you see, I have been given an extension on my lease.

JOE (*flatly*). How wonderful, Louis. Congratulations.

OBLIGING BOB.
     Dear Heaven, such a rancid life,
     While I defile the dinner plate…'

LOUIS. Thank you, Bob. (*Then, to* JOE.) I assume from your choice of clothes this morning that you are still in conflict with your wife.

JOE. Louis, there have been some goings-on since you were taken to your bed.

FANNY. No need to trouble Louis now, Joe. He is only just arisen.

LOUIS. And from your corrugated eyebrows, I deduce that you are somehow at the centre of these goings-on, Joe.

JOE. Well…

FANNY. Don't concern yourself with them, Louis. All will be well well well. Won't it, Joe?

JOE. Of course, as soon as Belle will allow me to retrieve my things, I will be able to ensure that all is well again.

FANNY. Joe, don't strain poor Louis! What a thing to do on a day such as this.

JAVA enters with a tray.

LOUIS. Ah! My banana-pudding girl! (*To* JAVA.) What's this?

JAVA. I bring you two spoons. One big, one small. So you can make banana castle in your pudding.

LOUIS (*delighted*). Ah, my little frangipani! My bonnie lass! And I will make a castle in my pudding, a big one! But what shall I use for a moat? (*He knows the answer.*)

JAVA. Coconut milk! Here!

She produces a jug of coconut milk and pours it on.

LOUIS (*sheer joy*). Oh! Oh! Oh. Oh. Thank you, Java, thank you. And how is cook's bad foot?

JAVA. Oh, is nearly better now.

LOUIS. Send him my best regards and tell him I'll come and see him this afternoon. Oh, and Java?

JAVA (*turning with a smile*). Yes, Mr Stevenson?

LOUIS. Mana'ao Tupapa'o [*pronounced 'Man-ow Tooper-pow'*]. The spirits are watching over you.

JAVA. Tch, tch!

JAVA exits, smiling.

FANNY. Your eyes were made for seeing, Louis, not ogling.

JOE. If I could speak with you, Louis...

FANNY. Not now, Joe. Could you please wait outside on the verandah. I will speak with you later.

LOUIS (*saying grace*). Lord have mercy on this island, bless our forest house, and when the period of our stewardship draws to a close, when the bond of family is to be loosed, let there be no bitterness of remorse in our farewells.

OBLIGING BOB *and* FANNY. Amen!

LOUIS (*playing with his food*). And now, I shall lower the draw-
bridge, thereby damming up the moat! (*He eats a mouthful.*)
Oh! There are so many things which make life worth living,
but the taste of banana pudding, so redolent of the nursery, is
an affirmation of commonality for all humankind! The
thought of all the myriad banana puddings on these islands
alone, which might at this very moment be being tasted, a sort
of communion of banana-ness, I fancy. And when one con-
templates the taste of puddings yet to come! Puddings from as
far away as… the Gilbert Islands! Hawaii! (*Which he pro-
nounces correctly, with two glottal stops: 'Hawa-i-i'.*) San
Francisco! Nay, London! Even, may I humbly posit, banana
puddings in Edinburgh itself! When one thinks of this, one is
overcome with a kind of refulgent effervescence, as if satu-
rated, then rinsed with the pulsy, pregnant… banana-y taste of
life itself! Ooooh! (*He takes another mouthful. Then, turning
to* JOE.) Joe? The first duty in this world is for a man to pay
his way, and when…

JOE. Of course.

FANNY. Louis, stop – Joe, you can wait on the verandah until
Louis has finished eating.

LOUIS. …when that is quite accomplished, he may plunge into
what eccentricity he likes, but emphatically not until then.
And now, a catapult attack! Ftang!

*He plops the back of the smaller spoon against the 'wall' of
his banana-pudding castle. Pudding flies out over the table.*

Oops. Sorry, my dear.

FANNY. Louis, you must leave the admonishments and matters
of real life to me. What little is left of your constitution must
be preserved for the world of the imagination and the inkwell.
You must work. For all our sakes, you must work. Belle will
be returning soon, I'm sure, and will be happy to take dicta-
tion. How is your hand?

LOUIS. Oh, we need the money, eh? Is that it? I believe I will
inhabit the spacious firmament for a short while yet. But when

I am capable of dictating to Belle once again, I shall return to my study of the anthropology of these islands, and not to the next boys' adventure book which I know you would prefer me to embark on.

FANNY. No more treatise on Polynesian races, Louis! Please!

LOUIS. Oh, for goodness' sake! Rumbustious pirates may well sell more, but the number of purchases is no measure of the validity of a book.

FANNY. Louis, you cannot blame the entire world and all your friends if they prefer tales of adventure to fanatical tracts on the politics and peoples of these islands, most of which they've never heard of.

LOUIS. You know, the last time Colvin deigned to write a letter to me, he asked whether I would consider returning to the Northern Hemisphere to 'fulfil my earlier promise'. As if my constitution were able to choose in which climate it can survive.

FANNY. Sidney Colvin is a dear friend who only wishes for your happiness...

LOUIS (*with disgust*). 'Have you perhaps another *Suicide Club* in you...? Or even another *Jekyll and Hyde*...?'

OBLIGING BOB. Oh yes! That one I liked! Very much indeed!

LOUIS. Thank you, Bob.

OBLIGING BOB. The uncanny doubleness of the separable self!

LOUIS. Well... yes... it was...

OBLIGING BOB (*acting out Jekyll's transformation into Hyde*). 'This repugnant evil, too, was... myself!'

FANNY. Perhaps we should discuss this later, when Joe has gone.

LOUIS. I had become an insurance liability, Joe. That was the rub.

JOE. Yeah. I guess you're kinda stuck here.

LOUIS. Yes. I can never go home. This is my home.

OBLIGING BOB. The duality of the human soul! The darkness and the light! The good and... the evil...!

FANNY. That will do, Bob!

LOUIS. If my choice is between the suicide of a return to the grey dampness of our shabby civilisation, or committing publishing suicide by staying here where the horizon is wide, well – what would you have me do, Fanoola?

FANNY. Perhaps Sidney merely meant to remind you that your readers, who love you so well, are all in the Northern Hemisphere – apart from Obliging Bob, of course – and they don't care so much to know how high above sea level Tahiti is.

LOUIS. Eight thousand feet. While our own beloved Mount Vaea is a mere twelve hundred feet, and, this being a low-high island, is also less sheer.

FANNY. You're not a geography teacher, Louis. You're a storyteller. Or were. A teller of tales. The Tusitala.

LOUIS. You attack me because I respect these islanders, and I write in defence of their religions and their customs – yes, even that of the eating of human flesh.

OBLIGING BOB. Steady on, old chap! Not had that round here for at least three years, don't y'know!

LOUIS. Maybe not, Bob, but to hell with my beloved Northern readers, who have not the stomachs to hear the truth about their scabrous Empire and its shamefully corrupt authority, which Fanny and I, who have travelled across it, can testify is in the hands of second-rate racketeers, shabby copra thieves, buccaneers, nefarious missionaries and assorted broken white folk living on the bounty of the natives.

FANNY. You are beginning to sound pompous and overblown. You've lost your lilt.

LOUIS. No I haven't. I have not lost my lilt.

FANNY. You have.

LOUIS. Anyhow, a lilt is tiresome and tricksy. And Lloyd agrees with me.

FANNY. No he most certainly does not! He would like more Highland tales.

LOUIS. Yes he does. He told me so himself.

FANNY. You think I would not know the opinions of my own son?

LOUIS. Perhaps you should try speaking with him once in a while. It is not enough merely to have given birth to him twenty-odd years ago.

FANNY. Uhh! You have always been so thick with Lloyd!

LOUIS. I should have thought a mother would be happy for such closeness to develop between her children and their stepfather.

FANNY. Louis! Let me deal with Joe! He is my son-in-law, it is for me to keep him from dragging us down. You are too good, Louis. You are a too-good fish swimming in a big, bad ocean...

LOUIS. Each of us has two sides, wife. Like the moon. The side we show to the world and the Other Fellow. The one we never show. The darker side. The one which, of course, makes much more interesting stories.

FANNY. I think it's best that the darker side of you is kept hidden. Away from public view. If you're talking about publishing further tales of your own depravity. Not what is expected of you, Louis. The prostitute book was no good.

LOUIS. I cannot let you interfere again, Fanny.

FANNY. That was your choice at the time. I gave my opinion, that was all. You asked my opinion on it, and I gave you it...

LOUIS. ...with an insistence bordering on the dominant. I will never let you make me burn a manuscript again, however lewd or upsetting its content. It's gone for ever, that one.

An embarrassed silence. OBLIGING BOB *interests himself in the flower arrangements.*

You see, Joe, what it is to marry a woman years older than oneself and thus remain, in her eyes at least, for ever a child.

He is finishing up his banana pudding and licking both spoons.

So, what is it this time, Joe? How much do you need?

FANNY. Louis! We can no longer afford...

LOUIS. My health may be jimmy, but I'll no' be scupper'd in ma' ain hoom by a lassie.

FANNY. I can't tolerate ingratitude, Louis. You have subsidised enough. Joe owes you his body, his soul and his boots...

LOUIS. ...and the soup that he wipes on his moustache. But, my darling McFanny, since I have fallen into a kind of patriarchal respectability and am the chief provider round here, I think it is down to me to organise and determine the moral running of my household. Hard is the lot of he who has dependents!

FANNY (*boiling over, somewhat hysterically*). Joe! Out on the verandah! Louis, finish your breakfast!

Pause while all three men wait to see if FANNY *is going to calm down or get more hysterical.*

LOUIS. So, how will you manage, Joe, when I am gone? Eh? No more handouts? I trust you will be careful, then, not to take for granted the equilibrium of your mother-in-law and learn to treat her with a calming voice. As I do.

FANNY (*controlling herself again*). Obliging Bob, will you find Joe a seat on the verandah, please?

OBLIGING BOB. But of course, Mrs Stevenson.

LOUIS. Bob, don't go too far, I do want to see the road to my tomb as soon as I can muster force.

OBLIGING BOB. I will tell everyone you're coming! They will be so happy!

JOE. I'll take a walk. Really. I have nothing particular to do this morning, as usual. I can wait.

FANNY. There are a thousand things you could be doing to help.

OBLIGING BOB. This way, Mr Strong.

JOE. All right, Bob. Perhaps you could oblige by letting go my elbow?

OBLIGING BOB *ushers* JOE *out with him.* OBLIGING BOB *and* JOE *exeunt.*

FANNY. Louis, he is a devil. You said so yourself.

LOUIS. Perhaps in the short time allotted to me until the Big Day, I could spend some happy hours with gardening. How many jungly acres of the estate have we cleared since we got here? Ten? Eleven? We must work harder.

FANNY. It just keeps growing back. No matter how much I fight it down, it… just keeps growing back.

LOUIS. Yes. However one struggles to contain the dark undergrowth, one so often finds that one has created the very evil one was seeking so hard to suppress. It's like the human soul. Nevertheless, now that I have this temporary respite from the inevitable, we must return to our land with renewed vigour. Personally I would be happy to do nothing but clearing away jungle for the rest of my days. There is nothing in the world as interesting as weeding. Nothing.

FANNY. You musn't do the gardening, Louis, it is too depressing. The heat, the insects, the islanders. It will make you ill again. I will do the gardening. Even though it gives me headaches.

LOUIS. So. What must I do, Fanny, for the rest of my days? Whistle in my cage?

FANNY. Do you understand what we endure here on your behalf? I hate the sea. And am I never allowed to be sick? Only you? I have had a headache for seven weeks now!

LOUIS. Oh, my dear girly, have you?

FANNY. I am stifled by this cloying sensual heat, these endless… smiling faces! Everywhere. Asking you for advice. Taking up your time. Which you are too generous with, Louis. Too generous.

LOUIS. Tender comrade! Wife! You are my teacher. I will do only as you recommend.

FANNY. Although you may take delight in imagining yourself the Laird of some Scotch clan, Louis, we are not in the Highlands now.

During the following, LOUIS *takes out a pouch of rolling tobacco and rolls himself a cigarette which makes him cough a little at the first drag. They stop momentarily for this but are in mid-conversation and neither notice that, possibly, smoking might not be the best thing for* LOUIS' *lungs.*

LOUIS. But I am a Scotsman. It is not by chance that we have settled here amongst this rugged island scenery; so much is similar between our current residence and the homes of my ancestors.

FANNY. Ancestors? You come from the city of Edinburgh, Louis. There was a street lamp over your front door.

LOUIS. But as I lie awake at night, it is so easy to imagine I have slipped ten thousand miles away and am anchored in a Highland loch, and that when the day comes it will show pine and heather, and roofs of turf sending up the smoke of peats.

FANNY. But what about the coconut palms? Endless coconut palms. Not a lot of them in Scotland.

LOUIS. Yes, but it's the people that make the place. And the working people of these parts suffer in the same way that the rugged clansmen of the Highlands do. The greedy English arm of Empire extending to scoop up all in its grasp.

FANNY. But the Highlands are cold, Louis. Very, very cold. Here we sweat in our underclothes and faint for lack of a breeze.

LOUIS. Fanny, must you contradict on everything?!

FANNY. We are here for the climate, Louis, which is the only way for you to survive. It is my vocation to protect you from your own ill health. My vocation in life.

LOUIS. I think you should allow me to be master of my own metabolism! Allow me that at least!

FANNY. Even though raw fish and coconut is not at all to my taste, I exist on a diet of it because it keeps you well. That is my only fulfilment.

LOUIS. Please stop trying to take my illness away from me, Fanny! It is mine! It's the one thing I know I have. My notoriety may be more the result of a remarkable amount of hard work than any particular talent, but the weakness of my lungs is me. I have learned to live with it since I was eight, you cannot have me without it!

FANNY. If it weren't for you, I would simply pack up my sewing machine and book the first passage to San Francisco!

LOUIS. Well, very soon, no doubt, when I fizzle out, that is exactly what you will be able to do.

Pause. He puts his arm up to comfort her. She ignores it.

Well, I'll... go and look at my grave, then. Where's my velvet jacket?

JAVA enters to clear the table. FANNY goes to get LOUIS' velvet jacket.

Ah! Java! My bread-and-butter beauty! A miracle of successful womanhood in every line. When I look at you I am glad that I am sick and overworked!

JAVA reaches over the table to clear his bowl. FANNY comes down to help LOUIS on with his velvet jacket.

Such strong knees on the girl, wouldn't you say? Like masts astride a floating hull.

FANNY. Well, enjoy as much as you like now, because she'll be gone by the end of the week, won't you, Java? (*Then, to LOUIS.*) Are you ready?

LOUIS. I am. What is her crime?

During the following, FANNY helps LOUIS to stand, and after a few seconds catching his breath, clinging onto the table edge, she helps him into his velvet jacket.

FANNY. She's costing us more than her usefulness. Leaving her oil lamp on all through the night, thus draining our resources unnecessarily.

LOUIS (*looking kindly at JAVA, who looks at the floor*). Leaves the light on all night, eh?

FANNY. Yes, and then, for lack of proper sleep, she ambles through the day half-senseless.

LOUIS. Perhaps she fears a visit from her ancestors, her Tupupa'o. There's nothing a dead Samoan forebear likes so much as a darkened room and a frightened girl.

FANNY. Well, we're not paying her dead forebears, just Java.

LOUIS. But Fanny, have you considered that, from our poor maid's perspective, the house is haunted by a thousand of her dead relatives who jostle and crowd into every shadow, their icy fingers itching to seize her and tear her like a paper doll at every lapse of vigilance?

FANNY. Well, if they would maybe sweep the rooms or do the laundry every so often, then maybe we could come to an arrangement.

LOUIS. It would seem ignoble to dismiss her on the grounds of her religion. Isn't that so, Java?

JAVA. No, Mr Stevenson. I believe in God now. He make Adam and Eve. He give them cargo. Of can meat, iron tools, rice in bags and matches. But they done Sin. So Jesus, he is kidnapped in Tuamotu Islands. So we must be good or Jesus will not be come again to Samoa.

LOUIS. Crikey! Now there's a story! But a no more far-fetched one than what my father held to be true. He was a staunch Presbyterian Unionist, Java. Staunch.

FANNY. That is all, Java.

JAVA. Yes, Mrs Stevenson.

JAVA *collects the dishes*.

LOUIS. I let him down.

JAVA. Mr RLS?

LOUIS. Yes, Java.

JAVA. Your papa, he been come here too much when you ill coughing.

LOUIS (*surprised and affected by what* JAVA *has said*). Did he, by Christ! (*Then, to* FANNY.) You see, my dear…?

FANNY. Java!

JAVA *exits with the dishes.*

LOUIS. I rendered his life a failure. My father. That's what he told me. Before he died.

FANNY. Whatever you say, my darling. She's leaving on Friday.

LOUIS. I rendered his entire life a failure. That's what he said. Well, he shouted it, rather, in a tone bordering on the melodramatic.

FANNY. Now, you are not to descend onto the lawn. Bob must show you everything from the vantage point of the end of the verandah.

FANNY *takes* LOUIS *to the door, holding him carefully by the elbow.*

(*Calling to* OBLIGING BOB *at the door.*) Obliging Bob! Tusitala is here!

LOUIS (*at the door*). Aaaah! The smell of the Pacific! An intoxicating mix of ylang-ylang, woodsmoke and drying coconut meat!

OBLIGING BOB *comes to the double doors, and takes* LOUIS *off* FANNY.

OBLIGING BOB. Jolly good show! Jolly good show!

FANNY. Don't take him beyond where I can see him.

LOUIS. And ssshhh…! Yes! The ceaseless requiem of the surf hanging on the ear like the 8.13 from Paddington!

OBLIGING BOB *exits with* LOUIS, *leading him further into the blinding white sunlight.*

FANNY *goes to the table where* LOUIS *has left his rolling tobacco and rolls herself a cigarette.* JOE *re-enters, sulkily.*

FANNY. Time's up, Joe. You're outta here by four o'clock this afternoon. Understood?

JOE. Well… perhaps when Belle returns from Apia she could help…

FANNY. No. No more Belle. Leave my daughter alone from now on, buster. You may have messed up your own life, but time to get out of hers. As of four o'clock this afternoon. You get it?

JOE. I was gonna say maybe Belle might let me retrieve my things from my quarters...

FANNY. No. Joe. No.

JOE. ...when she returns from Apia? Is that... all right?

FANNY. I'm sure Obliging Bob will oblige if you ask him nicely before four. And those are not your quarters, they are Belle's.

JOE. Yes, but I need to sort through my things, you know? There are... there are items to return to the safe.

FANNY. Items? What items? When did you gain access to the safe?

JOE. Well, Louis was unwell and...

FANNY. And how did you come by the keys? What imbecile entrusted you with the spare keys?

JOE. No. No. Belle thought it would be a good idea if she helped me to... She is still my wife...

FANNY. Belle had the keys off Louis?

JOE. Oh yeah. He trusts her with everything.

FANNY. Oh. What items did my daughter steal for you, Joe? Come, we'll make an inventory. Now.

FANNY *reaches in her skirt pocket and produces keys on a string. She marches across to the large safe, with her cigarette hanging on her lip.*

JOE. Mrs Stevenson, I... may have acted foolishly, but the pressures on me – not just financially – I had hoped for – Belle and I had hoped for – some kind of ongoing help... with all enterprises failing...

FANNY. My husband is not, nor never has been, a well man, Joe Strong. He is weak, as you know. And, leaving aside our financial precariousness, his position on the island is such –

well, the respect he's held in means that you can expect no
help from us with the woman. Nor with a child if there is one.
Although I shouldn't think you have the spunk in you. You
sack of phlegm! I will never understand how you fathered
little Austin. (*Opening the safe*.) Now, let's see.

JOE. I should have thought Louis might have been the one to
understand my position.

FANNY. And you're not to talk to Lloyd, at all! Do you understand? Not even to talk to him! Leave both of my children
alone!

JOE. Louis understood Father Damien, didn't he?

FANNY. Father Damien dedicated his life to the lepers, Joe.
What have you done with yours?

JOE. I mean, when Father Damien's choice of women was dis-
covered, Louis supported him then...

FANNY. Joe. Father Damien is a good man. That's why Louis
supported him. Louis is a good man. (*Looking in the safe*.)
Well, half the whisky's gone. Can't say I'm too surprised at
that. I should think you'll have a job returning that 'item'.
Likewise two bottles of wine, the claret. Louis will be beside
himself.

JOE. So, what's the good man gonna do, huh? Stage one of his
'family trials' and make me stand in the corner? Forfeit a pig
or two?

FANNY (*a new thought occurs to her*). How much money have
you had Belle steal for you? How much did you need to pay
off the woman's family?

FANNY *takes a cashbox from inside the safe*.

JOE. Dear mother-in-law, how low do you imagine I have sunk?
Please...

FANNY. There's been no sinking going on here! You were low
when I met you, you are low now, Joe Strong! Low, low, low!
(*She is still smoking, counting the money from the safe*.)
Hmph! So, just the alcohol so far. Unexpectedly, our small
reserve of cash is untouched...

She puts the money back, satisfied that it is all in fact there, then puts the box back in the safe.

JOE (*agitated now*). If you will just allow me to retrieve the… things from upstairs, I swear I can make all things good! Reparation! I could be back downstairs before Louis returns from looking at his damn road to paradise, he need not be disturbed by this in any way. Damn you! Always in my way!

FANNY. Aaaaah! (*She has been searching through the safe.*) The pistol!

FANNY *turns with a pistol in her hand, which she swivels expertly – Western-style – round her finger and then points threateningly at* JOE.

Where's the other pistol, Joe? What did you take it for?

JOE. I… needed to be sure… There are people… Things have gone so wrong for me…

FANNY. Yes they have, Joe. Four o'clock, Joe. No speaking with either of my children, no retrieval of any belongings and the second pistol returned to me. With all bullets intact. On second thoughts, you wanna use it on yourself before then, that's acceptable, so long as you don't do it here and so long as you have made arrangements to have the thing cleaned and returned to me by four o'clock, as I mentioned.

LOUIS *enters from the verandah, helped by* OBLIGING BOB, *who stands at his elbow.*

LOUIS. Superlative, Bob! That's the word for it! Really. It will be my right royal road to nirvana! (*Noticing the situation he has just walked in on.*) Oh. Are you going to kill Joe, Fanny? Belle might never forgive you.

FANNY. No, my darling. Merely giving him a lesson in the uses of firearms…

FANNY *puts the pistol away and closes and locks the safe.*

LOUIS. Oooh. Listen well, Joe. My wife is a crack shot, don't you know.

FANNY. …should he ever wish to do us all the favour of putting an end to himself.

OBLIGING BOB. Mrs Stevenson, Joe, I beg you to desist! How to explain such an act to the authorities. Mr Stevenson...?

LOUIS. There are so many more reasons *not* to commit suicide than there are to do it. Apart from the overriding fact that it's a mortal sin and you run the risk of some kind of damnation – possibly eternal – there is the downright mediocrity of the act. Don't even think of it, Joe.

JOE. It's good to see you standing up again, Louis. God is obviously on your side. The benefactor's Benefactor.

LOUIS. I'm not so sure that is true, but thank you all the same, Joe. And what a scene of superabundant sex there is out there! It's as well the Lord did not choose our garden for His story of Genesis and Original Sin. Dear Eve would have been banjaxed for choice! Adam might have forgone the simple blandness of the Northern apple for the exotic pleasures of our guavas, our mangoes and our pawpaws! One wonders, would Christianity have caught on so, had it been based on the premise of an avocado of good and evil? I must sit now.

    OBLIGING BOB *helps* LOUIS *into the room and, with* FANNY, *sits him down.*

FANNY. So long, Joe. Louis needs to rest now.

    LOUIS *coughs again. Everyone stops to see if it will develop. It doesn't. They carry on.*

LOUIS (*through coughs*). I know that things are not right with you, Joe. Your dress sense alone could tell a man that. If you can give me a little time to resuscitate, perhaps you and I could talk things through as a couple of men, alone, as we have done before. The more you can confide, the more there is to forgive.

FANNY. No. Louis, some things cannot be solved with conversation, however fair and frank it may be. Sometimes a more forceful hand is needed. Bob? Louis must have peace. His equilibrium must not be further interfered with.

OBLIGING BOB (*going to* JOE, *politely but firmly*). Yes, Mrs Stevenson. Mr Strong? Care for a stroll along the jolly old boardwalk?

OBLIGING BOB *goes to the doors and waits for* JOE *to join him there.*

LOUIS. My dear Fafine, just because I have been conversing with the dead these last few days, it should not follow that I am no longer able to balance in the swell of family mishap.

An awkward pause. JOE *does not move. Suddenly, there is a single crack of thunder.*

Joe, I think perhaps you have stayed this morning longer than your current standing in this family warrants. Perhaps you could absent yourself now, as Fanny has asked you, before the whole day goes jing-bang.

OBLIGING BOB (*indicating the exit*). By jingo! If there isn't going to be rain again before the sun gets over Tom Daly's yardarm!

FANNY (*dismissing him*). Yes. Thank you, Bob.

OBLIGING BOB. Thank you, Mrs Stevenson. Mr Stevenson.

OBLIGING BOB *exits.*

JOE. I need to collect my things. My paintings. Brushes. Other items. From Belle's room.

LOUIS (*irritated*). Well, please do so. If you go up there now you could be gone before she returns. No need to create a further scene.

FANNY (*through sobs*). Louis! I have already said! I told him he must not go up there!

JOE (*to* LOUIS). Exactly right. I won't be long.

FANNY. Must you always take everything away from me!

JOE *goes to the bottom of the 'stairs' and starts to climb. Then...*

JOE. ...Louis *is* writing a new story, Mrs Stevenson. Nearly finished in fact. A romance. An adventure tale set on the high seas. A real swashbuckler. That will, no doubt, be very popular. But only Belle knows it, because it's Belle that Louis is really close to, isn't it? We all know. It's Belle who he spends all his time with.

LOUIS. Oh dear.

JOE (*to* LOUIS). All day, you sit there with my wife. Dictating. (*To* FANNY *again*.) Every word of the bold new story – told first to Belle. And then to Java, of course. His native muse…

> JOE *exits up the 'stairs'.* LOUIS *and* FANNY *are left alone.* FANNY *looks accusingly at* LOUIS.

LOUIS. I am not all good, as you describe me. Not good. I am wicked too. In my imagination I have murdered – serially. I have sucked on the bones of my victims, I have sodomised. I have raped. Is imagining such things a sin? Is writing them down?

FANNY. No. But not telling me about it is.

LOUIS. It's an adventure story, Fanny. Yes. That's all there is to it.

FANNY (*shouting*). So, why didn't you tell me?

LOUIS. Your screechiness made it impossible, Fanny. Some days it ain't you I'm dealing with any longer.

> FANNY *would like to hit him, but cannot as he is too fragile.*

FANNY. You sonofabitch!

> *No reaction from* LOUIS.

You… you cripple! You half-a-man!

LOUIS. Wrinkled prune! Thing of dust! You see? You see how nasty I can be?

> *They stare at each other, upset.* LOUIS *calms down enough to quote one of his children's rhymes at her.*

> When I am grown to man's estate,
> I shall be very proud and great.

FANNY (*still trembling*). If you weren't half-dead already, I'd kill you!!

LOUIS.
> And tell the other girls and boys,
> Not to meddle with my toys.

FANNY. Feeble! Feeble! And I never did like that *Child's Garden of Verse* anyway! Rubbish! A smug, sentimental…

LOUIS. …mawkish, facile, contrived… best-seller. Yes, I agree. Oh! What's that? (*He puts his hands to his head*.) Ow! *Ow!* My head! My head!

FANNY. What is it? Louis? What do I do now?

LOUIS. Like nothing before! Aaagh! (*He is in great pain*.) Do I look strange?

FANNY. Erm… I'll get a remedy. Can you wait while I go upstairs to the pharmacy? Louis? (*Then, calling*.) Java?!

LOUIS. This is not the lungs! What an inconceivable pain! Urgh!

FANNY *rushes to ring a little bell which is on a small table*.

FANNY. Java? Come quickly, RLS is not well! Wait here, my love, while I fetch a balsam!

FANNY *exits hurriedly up the 'stairs'*.

LOUIS. Ooof! This is somewhat different! This is not me!

LOUIS, *standing centre stage, suddenly vomits a large quantity of blood down his white shirt. He is convulsed with pain and sinks to his knees*.

Uhh! Vomiting? Oh, girly! (*He calls weakly*.) Years of preparation wasted. Fanny?

FANNY *appears behind him, on the landing if there is one, holding a jar and a sachet*. LOUIS *is directly downstage of her. She does not see his blood-stained shirt*.

FANNY. Louis? Are you coughing, Louis?

LOUIS. No. No. Not coughing. My head…

FANNY *rushes back up and off*.

FANNY (*offstage*). Joe! Joe! Come quickly! Louis is not well! Joe!

JAVA *enters. She is frightened to see* LOUIS *covered in blood*.

LOUIS. Java, my angel! (*Seeing* JAVA *frozen to the spot.*) Java, Java, Java. Oh, Java! The times I could have spent with you, Java…! (*He smiles at her.*) Uhh! Here it comes again!

LOUIS *vomits blood again, this time over the floor.* JAVA *stands and stares at him. He beckons but she will not come and comfort him.*

I am not a devil, Java, just a man. What cunning spirits you have on these islands. I was looking in another direction entirely… I promise not to come back and haunt you, girl… well, not too often anyhow… Ha! I'm frightened now… I'm not ready… Oh, Father, I'm sorry!

JAVA *is frightened. There is a second crack of thunder.*

Don't go, Java… What are we, Java? Where am I going now…? And…

With one last heaving breath, LOUIS *dies. After a moment,* JAVA *is joined by* OBLIGING BOB, *who has taken off any colonial-style clothing and appears more like an islander. Together they take down rush matting from the walls and cover* LOUIS *in tapa cloths, so that initially he is lying with his elbows on top of the drapes, as he was in the opening scene.*

On or behind the walls from which they have removed the rush matting, shapes of Tiki ritual statues start to appear. The house is disappearing to create a more island atmosphere.

It starts to rain on the corrugated-iron roof. One drop at first then a steady drumming which gets louder and louder until, eventually, it becomes the Maori drumming from earlier.

Finally, OBLIGING BOB *and* JAVA *cover* LOUIS *in one last rush mat so he is completely concealed.* OBLIGING BOB *and* JAVA *leave.*

After a few seconds the drumming stops abruptly and the actor who played LOUIS *sits up, suddenly, as if from a nightmare. He is no longer covered in blood. He is no longer* LOUIS, *he is now* PIGO. *The rain continues on the corrugated-iron roof.*

PIGO (*waking with a start and taking in his surroundings*). Uh!
Temana?! Temana! I had another dream! I dreamed I was
dead. And they were carrying me to consecrated ground! A
Catholic burial! Aagh! Temana? Temana, wake up! I had a
bad dream.

TEHA'AMANA *sits up in the bed beside him. She is played
by the actor who played* JAVA, *and is now in a Tahitian
sarong with flowers.*

TEHA'AMANA. What is it now? Old man.

PIGO. I had another vision, Temana. Give my knees a rub like
you used to.

TEHA'AMANA. Huh.

PIGO. And could you bring me my sketchbook and a couple of
pencils so I can draw it while it's fresh…? Temana? It was so
vivid.

TEHA'AMANA. Get it yourself.

PIGO. Right. Hmmph. I will.

*He makes a half-hearted attempt to get up, but winces in pain.
He could now be standing or remain on the bed.*

I can't get it myself, Temana. How many sins does a man
have to notch up before the Church will – leave – him –
alone? Why do I bother with this eternal struggle against…
idiots… if they're going to bury me like a whitey in a grave-
yard… with Jesus? Eh? Bury me standing, put me on an iron-
wood skewer, or lay me on a Marai [*pronounced 'Ma-rye'*]
table like an islander. Temana? Don't let them bury me like a
long pig!

End of Act One.

ACT TWO

Tahiti, 1897.

A women's chorus chants a Polynesian hymn. The sound of tropical rain on a corrugated-iron roof engulfs the hymn-singing.

The stage space now represents the large studio room of Paul Gauguin, 'PIGO', and his Tahitian, common-law wife, TEHA'A-MANA. A large, untidy room with a rough wooden floor. Upstage centre is a small 'landing' area with two flimsy, rush-work doors off it, one of which leads to a tiny bedroom, and the other to a wooden front door, beyond which there are stairs down to ground level outside. The house is on stilts and, apart from the bedroom, this studio room is the only room of the house. The walls are made of rush-work panels with no glass in the window frames. There are hinged rush-work shutters, propped half-open by sticks. PIGO has made no money for over two years. There are empty bottles on the floor and perhaps a few clothes strewn about. There is virtually no furniture – anything of any value has been sold – the one fold-up chair and a few crates remain. An old guitar leans against a wall where there are also a few dirty, stretched-canvas frames stacked with some jars, brushes and wood-carving tools, but hardly a master artist's studio.

Spirits of the dead lurk in the shadows. It is not possible to dis-tinguish what might be one of PIGO's carvings from what might be island ritual masks or even ghosts. Again, luscious vegetation creeps in beyond the walls; this time, perhaps, more boldly.

It is night-time and dark. There is no lamp on. The tropical rain is thrumming on the rush-work roof.

After a few seconds, PIGO enters from the door which leads outside. He puts down a large bag and takes off his wet canvas cloak in the landing area before coming downstage in the semi-dark.

PIGO has suffered several injuries and illnesses in the last three years. He walks with a stick which has a carved phallus on the handle. He has never fully recovered from breaking his ankle in a fight two years previously and his lower legs are covered in eczema. He is in constant physical pain. He has dishevelled hair and a large zapata moustache. He wears the loose-fitting clothes of an islander.

PIGO. Temana? Are you there…? Mrs Penis?

He lights a match and looks around. The noise of rain begins to subside. He goes to the door and looks inside the bedroom, then lights another match and goes to get a bottle of oil out of his bag. During the following, he finds a lamp, fills it with the oil and lights it. Then another. The light is sickly yellow.

The mail boat was late. It went past the island by mistake and had to tack all the way back round. Took them two days. Imbeciles. Why are you in the dark?

He begins to unpack the rest of the contents of his bag; some rum, a bottle of absinthe, and a bottle of claret, which he opens.

I waited two days for the mail and had to talk to Father Lechery for seven hours about fencing and ditch-digging. They're going to sue me. The judge, the gendarme, the bishop. The whole, petty, bourgeois lot of them. I think they finally woke up to the fact that I am a bad influence.

TEHA'AMANA *appears at the bedroom door.*

TEHA'AMANA. You went to see Titi? You been with Titi?

TEHA'AMANA *is in her late teens but is not what we might think of as a teenager. Tahitian women were considered mature by thirteen. She is big-boned, good-looking and intelligent. She is four months pregnant.*

PIGO. I picked up my mail. I packed up my big painting and sent it off to Paris. The last one. I came back here. I walked all the way back with my legs. You may think it tiresome of me to mention it, but I am still in a lot of pain in my legs. How was he? Your loverboy? Did he do you good?

TEHA'AMANA. The men, they all went fishing. I was frighten.

PIGO. Did the ghost come back and touch you again?

TEHA'AMANA. That no funny. The light finished. We got no oil for the lamp. It was dark. I was frighten.

PIGO. So, it was the spirits of the dead who ravished your body? Is that what you're saying?

TEHA'AMANA. No. Not spirits.

During the following, PIGO *continues to unpack his bag. He takes out several boxes full of sachets, and then a box with syringes and ampoules in it.*

PIGO. They don't like what I wrote about them in their pox-ridden paper. And, strangely, they don't like the rude carving I made of the bishop. Ha! Now, they want to put me in prison. But that's not going to happen because first I'm going to kill myself.

TEHA'AMANA. You been with the fancy girls in Pape'ete [*pronounced 'Pappy-etty'*]? How much money you got now?

She gets up and goes upstage to where the new bottle of oil is (which was in PIGO's *bag), and starts to fill and light another lamp. The noise of the rain has gone.*

PIGO. Then you'll be happy. Then you can have all the boys, eh? All the fishermen. Temana? Come here.

TEHA'AMANA. No. You drunk.

PIGO. Not enough. Not yet. Come on, Temana. Come here. I'm back. Let me at least fail to arouse you. One last time.

TEHA'AMANA. No. Anyhows, in Tahiti, girl can have two husbands.

PIGO. Oh, really.

TEHA'AMANA. Yes. If first one boring.

PIGO. Am I boring?

Pause.

Hmm. Well, I have been called many names, but that's the worst. Insensitive, cruel, I could take. Evil, possibly. Anything but boring.

TEHA'AMANA. You old too.

PIGO. That one's quite hurtful too, actually.

TEHA'AMANA. And the pus on your legs smells too bad.

She has put down the lighted lamp. He tries to grab at her legs as she comes near, she pulls away.

PIGO. Well, I'm going to kill myself anyway, so don't think you can keep me alive just in the distant hope of having sex with you. Or even a welcoming hug.

TEHA'AMANA. If I unhappy, I leave. You said.

PIGO. Oh, not again, Temana. I beg you. (*Fatigued.*) Temana, Temana. Please. I need you. I want you. I need you... I adore you... (*He is running out of words.*) What would I paint if you go? What will there be for me to paint? Mmmm? Fruit? The gendarmes? The storekeeper? – You want me to paint Ben?

TEHA'AMANA *giggles at the idea of a painting of* BEN.

You want me to come all this way, throw off my degenerate European behaviours, cash in my life insurance, so I can paint pictures of a stinky American storekeeper, who smells so bad his whaleboat crew dropped him off here and never came back for him? Is that what you want?

She laughs now. She starts to brush her hair. He watches her.

What kind of paintings would I have had to send back to Paris, huh? 'Yankee too drunk to open can of beans'? 'Yankee shits his pants'?

TEHA'AMANA. 'Yankee wankee behind tree when Teha'amana washing.'

PIGO. Does he?

TEHA'AMANA. Yes. And he watch when you paint me and... (*She mimes a slob masturbating.*)

PIGO. You see! You can't leave me! Even when I'm dead. What about poor old Ben? You can't leave Ben.

TEHA'AMANA. So, you bring me present? New brush?

PIGO. I got you something. Not a brush. I have no money left. They're going to fine me two hundred francs and put me in prison for libel and for blasphemy. And for causing 'native unrest'. I told you. I'm finished. Just as well my last painting ever was a masterpiece!

TEHA'AMANA. I need new brush. Look.

She holds out the hairbrush to show him. He grabs her arm and pulls her close to him. He knows she will pull away, but he takes the opportunity to inhale the smell of her deeply. She pulls away.

PIGO. Oh, the smell of you! Fatal! Let me at least die inhaling you.

TEHA'AMANA. No. What you get in town then?

She brings his bag downstage and starts to take out the remaining contents and put them on the floor. She finds a bunch of papers and letters which she throws carelessly over the floor.

Letters… (*i.e. 'boring'.*)

PIGO *quickly grabs one of the letters and keeps it for himself, putting it carefully in his shirt or trouser pocket.*

PIGO. Not that one.

TEHA'AMANA *finds a bead necklace of polished nuts and shells. She shuns it and throws it on the floor.*

TEHA'AMANA. What's this?

PIGO. I thought it was beautiful so I got it for you.

TEHA'AMANA. Huh! This island stuff is cheap. You got all your medicines. You got booze. How much moneys for all that, eh?

PIGO. I thought we could share this rather nice bottle of Verbier as a sort of farewell? And I need the arsenic for my legs,

Temana, you know that. Besides, it is an appropriate ingredient for my suicide cocktail.

TEHA'AMANA. So, you got money for morphines and you got money for your arsenics. And you got plenty moneys for sending your masterpiece picture to Paris, France, but you got no little moneys for a brush, even. Or a dress. I want a dress like those Frenchies wear. All tight.

PIGO. You don't want that. You don't want that.

TEHA'AMANA. You tell me what I want?

PIGO. You can't want that. To look like some Parisian cocotte. Some white vahine [*pronounced 'va-heeny'*], with her whalebone corset squeezing her guts, and her pale elbows sticking out like sausage fat...

TEHA'AMANA. You got me no make-up? No powder stuff?

PIGO. ...with no grace, no... no muscularity, no sinuous connection with life. No fragrance.

TEHA'AMANA. You won't walk the street with me in Pape'ete. You ashamed of me.

PIGO. No no! It's not that! It's not you I'm ashamed of. It's the morally corrupt society I come from, with its bizarre ideal of slenderness which they all aspire to. It's my fault you want these things. I have corrupted you.

TEHA'AMANA. I want to go to the mayor's wedding in Pape'ete. They got a carnival.

PIGO. You know, they are trying to make Pape'ete just like the outskirts of Paris now. Everything lined up and neatly raked. There's even electricity! And a merry-go-round! A merry-go-round! It comes to this! The tribal dance of the civilised! Five cents a ride! It's the right time for me to finish. It's over. I will never paint again.

TEHA'AMANA. I like to see a carnival.

PIGO. You were happy, Christianity had not penetrated to this place, and now you want to be like an apple on a palm tree.

TEHA'AMANA. I want a wedding too. I want... a certificate.

PIGO. Why?

TEHA'AMANA. Not gonna say why. Need it. You ought to see why.

But PIGO *does not see, or chooses not to acknowledge her pregnancy.*

PIGO. You think that weddings make them happy? Only the rich marry. It's just another form of *droit de seigneur*. Nothing other than a sale. Like prostitution.

TEHA'AMANA. You give my mother a sewing machine to get me.

PIGO. Yes. That's also true, but…

TEHA'AMANA. I want a contract like them other vahines.

PIGO. But you have real beauty. Real grace. Fragrance. You can – you can dance. You can sing. You can move your hips, unlike those stuck-up, European, congealed… vomit-bricks. They're not real women. They're constructions. Anyone can buy a marriage contract cheap on any street in Pape'ete nowadays.

TEHA'AMANA. So why not you do it, then?

PIGO. Erm… fair point. Well, apart from the irritating fact that I never actually, really got round to divorcing Mette, you have to remember that I am a man who has absolutely no respect for their bourgeois institutions. I am a lone wolf, I do not howl with the pack. Anyway, what does it matter now? I'm going to be dead in a few hours… Ask Tiko to bury me quickly before they find out I'm gone. I don't want them giving me a Catholic burial, all right? I will not have it.

TEHA'AMANA. Teha'amana not enough talk-talk for you.

PIGO. No! Nonono… When I first saw you, it was I who hesitated. I who was timid in the face of you. Me, Pigo the old cock, tough and hoarse from so many women. A tough lump of horned rosewood which has become a piece of bruised fruit.

TEHA'AMANA. And now? When you see me now? Gone all big, huh? You see?

PIGO. Temana...! All the fire of the sun burns and shines in the splendour of your flesh and... and the magic of love sleeps in the night of your hair... and... erm... Oh, to hell with it, I can't do it any more.

TEHA'AMANA. I think you need your morphines now.

BEN *the storekeeper enters from the door which leads outside. He comes straight in without being invited.*

BEN *is a whaler-turned-trader who was indeed abandoned here by his whaleboat crew. He is an American in his thirties. Dressed as an islander, he has the tan of a man who has spent several years in the open air.*

BEN. Hello there, Pigo! The man! Hello, Mrs Penis! I thought I heard the sound of drinking!

PIGO. Ben! She says she's going to leave me!

BEN. That's because she can't keep up with you, Mr Penis, you're an animal, you're insatiable!

PIGO. Erm... if you insist. But I am fairly worn out by life now, and I have a broken ankle that will not heal and eczema all down my legs, so...

BEN. What did you get?

BEN *investigates the new bottles of alcohol.*

Oh, rum? I got plenty of rum in the store. Am I losing a customer here?

PIGO. Your rum is like water from a diaper. And you haven't got claret!

PIGO *uncorks the claret and takes a swig but does not swallow, then...*

(*His mouth full.*) And you haven't got absinthe!

An unswallowed swig of the absinthe.

And with this finer rum than yours, it makes...

He swills the drink around in his mouth like mouthwash, then swallows it all.

…a Suicide Cocktail!

BEN. Suicide Cocktail! Hurr, hurr! That's so funny! Look what I brought!

From his pockets, BEN *produces first a couple of glasses, one of which he hands to* PIGO, *and then a tin of fish, which he hands to* TEHA'AMANA.

– And… supper! Are you hungry, Mrs Penis? *Merci*, sir.

PIGO *has filled their glasses. The two men drink.*

Here's to native unrest! (*Pause*.) They're going to fry you, Pigo. They're going to bang you up and nail you down. Mrs Penis? Your makey-shaky man is a brave, crazy sonofabitch! Here's to no more taxes!

PIGO *has filled their glasses and they drink again.* TEHA'A-MANA *has taken the tin to where there is a knife and some bowls. She stabs at the tin to open it and puts whatever there is of the food into the bowls.*

TEHA'AMANA. He too lazy sonabitch. No bring good stuff from ship. No brush. No certificate.

BEN. Don't worry, Pigo. I'll take care of Temana while you're in the Calaboosa. We'll wait for you together, won't we, Mrs Penis?

PIGO. Thank you, Ben, for that reassuring thought.

BEN. That statue of the bishop! Woooo…!

PIGO. The wood carving…

BEN. Yeah, that carving? What made you think you could get away with that?

PIGO. I created a new movement in art, my boy. And don't you forget it. And these young painters nowadays are reaping the benefit of it. My symbolism is making a lot of money for creeps in Europe now…

BEN. Yeah, but six inches long! What was that a symbol of?

PIGO. I think I made my opinion of the bishop abundantly clear…

BEN. So, you won't be sending that one to your friends in Paris!

PIGO. Why should the natives respect a corrupt and venal Church? Why should they pay tax to have nothing but prejudice and prohibition forced on them? The young girls forced to cover themselves up, forced to go to missionary school...

BEN. When they could be hanging around your garden and forcing themselves into your bed!

PIGO. Well...

BEN *laughs lecherously.*

BEN. Tss tss. What's the most you ever had at the same time, Pigo man?

PIGO (*making it up*). Erm... er... three?

BEN. Three?

PIGO. Yes.

BEN. I mean, where do you... how did you...

PIGO. Fingers, cock and tongue left me one hand free to make a sketch of the event.

BEN. Ha! Ha! For the bishop! Ha! He'd love to see that one! So would I, actually!

BEN *goes towards the guitar which is leaning against the wall. On his way he fingers the canvasses stacked against a wall, trying to see what is on them.*

PIGO. It's not there, ladyboy. I destroyed it, of course. A mere sketch I can repeat from memory at any time I choose.

BEN. Wish I had a memory like yours!

BEN *returns with the guitar, strumming it absent-mindedly. He stops at the letters, still strewn on the floor. He sifts them with his toe.*

Oh. Was there mail for me?

PIGO. Ha! Ladyboy Ben, hoping beyond all empirical rationality that there is a sentient being on this earth who is remotely concerned with his existence – or can remember him, even.

You're in God's hands now, ladyboy. And God, as we all know, is a nineteen-year-old girl. Look at that!

He is referring to TEHA'AMANA, *who has arrived with bowls of food for* PIGO *and* BEN.

BEN. Mrs Penis? Did you know that you were God?

TEHA'AMANA. Oh, yes. I am Arii'oi [*pronounced 'Aree-oy'*]. I am gods. (*Then, more doubtfully.*) Before the missionaries come…

PIGO. You see. Whole religions destroyed to make way for a merry-go-round.

They eat. PIGO *tears open a sachet of arsenic and sprinkles it over his food like seasoning.* BEN *watches him, puzzled.*

Can I offer you some arsenic…? No?

PIGO *winces at the taste of the arsenic. There is a pause while they eat. Then, by way of explanation…*

I am going to kill myself today, you see. So this is a sort of Last Supper.

TIKO *enters, shouting.*

TIKO. Blasphemy! Blasphemy!

TIKO *is a man of about fifty, who has lived all his life on the island. He is* PIGO'*s neighbour. He is tattooed over his face. He is wearing non-Western clothes.*

PIGO. Good evening, Tiko. Or is it morning? What is the problem now?

TIKO. Oh my! Phew! Pigo? That damned rain has whooshed my house away! Whoosh! Right away! My house gone whoosh, right away all down the hill! That rain! Shoulda built my house better…! Never mind… I come and live here with you. 'Til we made a new one… Pigo?

During the following, TIKO *starts to take things out of his bag and lay them on the floor where he is going to live. He unrolls a mat to sleep on. Also out of his bag, he produces a couple of skulls and lays them out around his mat.*

PIGO. Whatever you say, Tiko. I only have a few hours to live, and so there will be plenty of room.

TIKO. Oh, my beloved Penis! You must be more careful. The church man, he is very angry now. So is the Big Guy on High.

PIGO (*to* BEN). Tiko, here, has eaten human flesh, haven't you, Tiko? Although he must deny it in front of the authorities.

TIKO. They no likey you blasphemy thing. You too much clever man, get me out of jail, thank you. But if I never been in Calaboosa, I never know the Gospel. I never know Jesus love me.

PIGO. I think the blame goes historically further back than Jesus, Tiko. Blame God. But that's not the point. The point is, what did it taste like, the human flesh? Chicken? Pork? Nectar?

TIKO (*smiling*). I never done it. I never eaten peoples. Never done long pig.

PIGO. Yes, you did. You did. You told me you did.

TIKO. Well, I not remember now.

PIGO. Maybe a drink will help it come back to you. Ben, make the man a cocktail!

TIKO. Naah! Naah! I don't do that drink no more. Jesus, he no likey.

PIGO. Look at this state of affairs! For millennia the people of this island have danced and sung. They've distilled palm wine until they were hog-whimperingly drunk. They have tattooed themselves and they have fucked – as legend would have it, they have fucked rather a lot actually. In a lot of entertaining ways and places. And now this old man is afraid to drink with us because Jesus might disapprove, and, more importantly, Jesus's representatives on earth will fine him ten francs. They will sling him in jail, they will take his house away.

TIKO. Naah. I told you. That rain took my house away. That rain gone everywhere. Oh, and the church got water so the roof come down. It's all punishment. The Big Guy must be angry with us.

BEN. Which church, Tiko?

TIKO. The proper church.

BEN. The Catholic on the hill?

PIGO. The Presbyterian? It's a shitty stick, the church. You never know which end to grasp it.

TIKO. The proper big church. The real church. You know.

PIGO. Which one, Tiko? The Congregational? The Huguenot? The Methodist? The Baptist? Episcopal? What a place this is. Seven churches and not a single chemist.

BEN. Here we have a Suicide Cocktail!

He offers a drink to TIKO.

TIKO. Naah. Temperance is sweet. Jesus loves me.

PIGO. Come on. Tiko. Drink.

TIKO. It's a bad thing.

PIGO. I heard you can finish off the contents of an entire palm tree and still walk the length of Puunaui'a [*pronounced 'Poona-we-a'*] Beach. Tiko?

Pause.

Tiko? Tiko? Have a drink with Pigo? Please?

TIKO. Oh, the hell. Here, use mine.

TIKO produces a jar of lethal-looking palm spirit. BEN and PIGO laugh, impressed. BEN downs the contents of the glass he was offering and puts it out for palm spirit. TIKO pours from the jar and grabs one of the glasses for himself.

PIGO. Now we descend! For the stultifying and theocratic reign of the Church, the sacerdotal guild of priests, the dogma of the immaculate conception, the abomination of fake relics and indulgences and the infallible authority of the Pope. Gentlemen – to blasphemy!

BEN. Blasphemy!

They drink. During the following, TEHA'AMANA fills another lamp, lights it and slowly makes her way to the bedroom door to leave.

(*Swallowing the palm spirit.*) Fwaaa! Ha! Oh boy! That's like fire! Like an engine room is on fire!

The jug is passed around. PIGO *notices what* TEHA'A-MANA *is doing and, although he joins in with the drinking, he keeps an eye on her.*

TIKO (*with a wheezy laugh*). Hoo! Haa! If we going to jail, let's dance!

PIGO. No, I can't. I'm in too much pain. But you dance, Tiko. Dance with your hips.

BEN *strums on the guitar and sways around. He sings a bit as well, picking up any words that are spoken and jumbling them in with a made-up Tahitian song.* PIGO *hauls himself up painfully and tries, stiffly, to move in time to the music towards* TEHA'AMANA.

BEN (*singing*). Maruru. [*'Thank you', prounounced 'Marooroo'*] Ia Orana. [*'Hello', prounounced 'Ya Rana'*] Nave nave fenua. [*'Land of sexual delight.'*] Te Faaruru. [*'I make you shake.' i.e. 'I fuck you.'*] Teine merahi noa noa [*'Now very fragrant.'*]

TIKO *dances like a jellied spider around the stage, singing and swivelling his hips.* TEHA'AMANA *is going to her room,* PIGO *follows her, but does not get there in time and the door is closed in his face. He pauses momentarily and moves on around the room. He picks up the little case of syringes and sits down to tourniquet his arm.* BEN *carries on playing quietly.*

(*Singing.*) Blasphemeee – immaculate conception – maruru – make shaky-shake…

BEN *stops playing for a moment.*

(*To* PIGO.) You need any help with that?

PIGO. Absolutely not.

BEN *plays again. The energy of* TIKO*'s dance is subsiding.* BEN*'s strumming becomes lazier. He is now sitting on the floor, slumped against a crate. Drinking as well as playing quietly.* TIKO *stops dancing and stands in the middle of the stage.* BEN *stops playing.*

TIKO. I did eat long pig, you know? I done eaten a white man.
When I was a boy. I eaten a white trader man. Oooh, he taste
good, that long pig. It made me strong. That's how I live so
old. Eating that long pig make me nice and strong and old.
Good teeth.

Pause.

Then BEN *resumes playing, quietly.*

BEN (*singing*).
        In the islands, I am told –
        There's a special kind of gold –
        Makes you strong and it makes you bold –
        Eat your neighbour and you'll grow old.

During the following, PIGO *succeeds in injecting himself with
morphine. Afterwards, he takes off the tourniquet and leans
back against the wall.*

PIGO. Well, Tiko my old friend, in a few hours I will be dead
and you will be welcome then to dig a long oven in the
ground and put me in it and cover me with hot banana leaves
and cook me up. Invite your island friends to share me out.
Although I shouldn't think I'll taste that good. Of arsenic and
absinthe, I should imagine. Just make sure they don't dump
me in consecrated ground.

BEN (*singing*).
        Ia Orana Ia Orana,
        Cover Pigo in banana,
        Cook him gently when he's dead,
        Taste the colours in his head.

BEN *goes to the closed door of the bedroom where* TEHA'A-
MANA *went. He serenades her through the door.*

        Te faruru. For goodness' sake!
        Temana lies in bed awake,
        I will make her shaky-shake,
        When Pigo's in his oven bake.

Suddenly BEN *stops. A woman has appeared. She has come
in from the door which leads outside, but she should seem to
have stepped from the shadows. She is* OTHERMOTHER.

She walks into the room carrying several bags. She puts the bags down, and pants. She smells the air and tuts, disapprovingly. They all look at her.

BEN. Hello?

OTHERMOTHER *is blind. She is mixed race and looks more like the spirit of the dead ancestor in Gauguin's* Manao Tupapao *than a live human being. She is dressed in a dark blue shawl.*

OTHERMOTHER. Is this the house of the picture man?

They all remain silent.

Who lives here?

TIKO. I live here.

OTHERMOTHER. Naah. You not the European. You smell like an islander to me, old man.

She stops for a moment and listens. She goes over to where PIGO *is – now standing up – and touches him to 'see' where he is. Her fingers pat over his face, then his shoulders.*

You the French man from Paris?

TIKO. No. He's an islander now.

OTHERMOTHER. Huh.

She feels down PIGO's *body to his trousers. She puts a hand inside his trousers and gropes around.*

Ha! What is that? What are you going to do with that?! Where are your scars, whitey?! You're no islander. You'll do nothing for a woman with that smooth thing. Ha! Pupa! You are the picture man.

PIGO. Who are you?

OTHERMOTHER. I am the mother of Teha'amana.

PIGO. No you're not. I know you're not.

Pause.

TEHA'AMANA *appears at the bedroom door. She stands and witnesses what is going on.*

I know the mother of Teha'amana, I gave her a sewing machine. I should have warned her it needed a new rotor belt, but apart from that it was in reasonable order.

Pause.

OTHERMOTHER. Teha'amana's got a lot of parents, monsieur. We share. I am her other mother.

TEHA'AMANA. Yes. Othermother. Now too late for you, old man.

PIGO. Oh.

OTHERMOTHER. Ia Orana, Teha'amana.

TEHA'AMANA (*sulkily*). Maruru.

Pause.

PIGO. Why are you here, by the way?

OTHERMOTHER. I come to live here. You got a new island baby coming soon.

PIGO. And you think I'm the father? Ha! That's rich!

OTHERMOTHER. We all look after the children here.

OTHERMOTHER *goes to* TEHA'AMANA *and touches her belly.*

Oah! It's a good 'un. Good baby coming.

TEHA'AMANA (*to* PIGO). See. You no hear too much what I say.

OTHERMOTHER *feels around the bedroom door and sniffs the air.*

OTHERMOTHER. Tch tch. You're going to have to clean this place up!

BEN (*still singing vaguely*). Shaky-shaky… baby baby?

PIGO. Will you shut up?

BEN. Right. That's me. I'm done. I'm going now.

BEN *picks up a bottle as if to leave, but loiters for a while. During the following, he makes his way to the stack of canvasses and starts to look through* PIGO*'s sketchbooks to see if he can find anything pornographic.*

PIGO. Well, Othermother, welcome to the house of pleasure, maison de orgasm. This is the pussy palace, villa vagina. We're all pussies here. What difference will one more pussy make?

Pause.

BEN. So, who do you think is the father, Pigo?

PIGO. Not me. Who cares?

TEHA'AMANA. Pigo! Pigo is. I want a christening in Pape'ete.

OTHERMOTHER *hisses at* TEHA'AMANA *to shut up.* TEHA'AMANA *retreats to her bedroom door and stands there, sulking in the shadows.*

OTHERMOTHER (*to* PIGO). You don't like babies?

PIGO. I have resolutely closed off my heart to sensitive feelings in order to preserve my artistic courage... everyone knows that.

OTHERMOTHER. So, a big price to pay, no?

PIGO. It has been necessary, for professional reasons, to keep any good there might be in me hidden, so that I can appear to the world as a monster.

TIKO (*smiling*). I have seventeen children... but I never been with a woman!

OTHERMOTHER. You can't have your bed there, old man. Put it in the corner.

OTHERMOTHER *kicks* TIKO*'s mat and skulls, and makes him move it to another part of the room. During the following,* PIGO *opens one of the sachets of arsenic from the cardboard box and quietly pours it into his drink. Then another, then another. He stirs the drink with his finger and drinks it down. He pours himself another drink and repeats the process.*

PIGO. As you can see, the accommodation may be somewhat cramped. I'm afraid as a great but undersubscribed artist, this 'studio' was all I could afford. But fear not, I do not intend to be using it. In fact, I am on the way out. My timing, for once, seems to have been immaculate.

OTHERMOTHER. So, you not going to stay around long enough to see your new child? That's good. You'll be in the way quite a lot for the first few years.

PIGO. It is a miscalculation to sacrifice yourself for a child. Every day ruined before it's begun, by their incessant early rising. A life of wiping babies' bottoms, what is the point of that?

OTHERMOTHER. Oh, you need a 'point'. Maybe you left your point in Paris.

PIGO. Yes. Maybe. However, with good health, independent work and regular sex, a man can pull through... and since I have none of those at present... and since my task is complete...

OTHERMOTHER. Oh, you got a task?

PIGO. Oh yes. A destiny. I have known for a long time what I was doing. Always.

BEN. Yes. He does. He knows what he's doing. He's killing himself.

PIGO. Thank you, Ben.

TIKO. Oh, my dear man! You crazy boy! What about the Holy Spirit? He's going to be jolly cross with you.

OTHERMOTHER. What was your task, monsieur?

PIGO. To let the darkness out. To turn the stone over. To expose the hypocrisy of its shiny façade.

OTHERMOTHER. Can you be more specific?

PIGO. All right. To exchange the useless Western model of beauty – created by the Greeks, incidentally – of harmoniously proportioned white men and women being impossibly good and healthy all over the place, to exchange them for asymmetrical, impure, pungent, blood-soaked prototypes. Yes.

BEN. Do you still have those photos from Port Said, Pigo?

PIGO. Yes, but you can't have them. Not even when I'm gone.

BEN. Just one?

PIGO. No. (*Then, to* OTHERMOTHER.) D'you want to see some photographs of fat women making shaky-shake in a hovel in Port Said?

OTHERMOTHER. *Non, merci, monsieur.* I have no eyes.

PIGO. Oh… (*Pause.*) Well, let me describe myself to you, madam. I was born with a disdainful face, and my years at sea have meant that my gaze has become frozen. Always looking towards the horizon, you see. To what is to come. You see, novelty is essential to stimulate the stupid buying public.

OTHERMOTHER *is tidying up and rearranging the seating. She pushes* PIGO *out of the way.*

My images of a primitive, black Eve frighten them. Their civilised, European Eve has a gap between her thighs like a pair of tweezers.

BEN *stands, swaying, too near* PIGO, *who wafts the air in front of his nose and coughs. The slow fade-up of dawn begins.*

BEN. It's not his fault there was no money to send to the other four children in Denmark. We all do our best, right? He left them his name, didn't you, Pigo? She's a bitch, their mother, right, Pigo?

PIGO. They never even wrote to me. Not once. 'Dear Papa' would have been enough. Their mother said only if I sent cash. What, am I supposed to buy their love?

BEN (*re: the guitar*). Hey, I'll bring this back tomorrow.

BEN *hovers near the door, with the guitar and a bottle, but still does not leave. He cannot face being alone in his own hut.*

Pause.

OTHERMOTHER. You should be careful, monsieur. You are a long way from your Adam and Eve now. Long way from your Greeks and Romans. We got different ancestors here, Mr Artist Man. We got different spirits in the dark. Different

Tupapa'o. Oooh, scary, yuh? Tell me, if you gone so native,
you so Tahitian, how come you still sending these to that Paris
place, huh?

OTHERMOTHER *nudges the canvasses stacked against the
wall. She picks one up and manhandles it, banging it against
the floor.*

PIGO. Not any more. I told you, my work is complete. My final
work was impossible to better.

OTHERMOTHER. So, this stuff's just wood and cloth now, uh?
This'd make good firewood, make good tapa cloth, make
good swaddling for the baby, yuh? Let's try, yuh?

OTHERMOTHER *puts her foot against one of the frames and
smashes it.* PIGO *fights his instinct to protect his work. But he
cannot and gets up to protect the canvasses.*

PIGO. Nooaah...

PIGO *has saved some of his canvasses from*
OTHERMOTHER. *It is morning outside and light is seeping
through windows. It increases rapidly in intensity during the
following.*

OTHERMOTHER. See? You not Tahitian. You... bourgeois.
Bourgeois!

TEHA'AMANA. Yes! Bourgeois man! You... hoodwinker! Hoodwinker! I stupid not see through you! You little cheater man!

TIKO (*remaking his bed*). Whoa! These island girls! Aren't they
something?!

TEHA'AMANA. You half-man! Whitey! Pupa! You too stupid!
Too stupid, too stupid!

BEN. I think she's trying to tell you that she's disappointed.

TEHA'AMANA. You no hoodwink me no more!

TEHA'AMANA *goes into the bedroom and slams the door
behind her.* OTHERMOTHER *clears the remaining mess to
one side and starts to take cooking pots out of her bags. This
area will be her kitchen.* PIGO *is slumping. A few scraggy
birds can be heard, no great dawn chorus.*

PIGO (*to* OTHERMOTHER). How nice it is to talk. I have no one to talk art to – or even French.

OTHERMOTHER. Actually, my father was from the London Missionary Society, don't you know? No one is simple.

PIGO. How paradoxical. And who would believe that I am descended from the Borgias of Aragon?! The viceroys of Peru?! I am, in fact, an Inca and when I die I shall return to the sun from whence I came, to be burnt in its glare...

OTHERMOTHER. No, you're no Inca. But with your European wings made of wax, you do fly too close to the sun. Like my father. He went to Rai'atea to spread the Gospel – that was his task – and they clubbed him to death and ate him on the beach. What was the point of that?

PIGO *has taken out the letter which he put in his pocket earlier and is looking at it.*

PIGO. My daughter died today. Aline. She had my mother's name.

BEN (*softly singing*). Today today, she died today...

TIKO (*sitting up*). Today? How you know she die today?

PIGO. Well, she died... (*He looks at the letter.*) ...six weeks ago, but I got the letter today. For me she died today.

TIKO. Oh. That bad. How she die?

PIGO. What does it matter?

TIKO. Well, if she not kill herself, then she not die in sin, then she gone to Jesus. They got big proper churches in France?

BEN (*continuing to strum gently*). Aline was Danish, Tiko. She lived in Copenhagen.

TIKO. Oh. That good?

PIGO. She died of pneumonia. She went to a dance and caught pneumonia and died in the hospital.

TIKO. So, dancing no good in Denmark then?

PIGO. That's right, Tiko, old chum. Danish dancing is execrable shit. It's almost impolite to produce anything but bad taste in Denmark! She was nineteen years old.

BEN (*laughing*). So, she was a god then?

PIGO. Aline is dead. God is dead. Her tomb is not in Copenhagen. That's a pretence. Her tomb is here with me. My tears are her flowers, they are living things.

OTHERMOTHER. Yes, here where the living eat the dead, the dead may eat the living too. Their spirits are all around us now, carved in the rock, in the shells, in the trunk of the Pandanu tree.

PIGO. I wonder that the world hasn't fallen apart, I have heard it creaking so often. To survive is torture.

PIGO *is incoherent and falls unconscious. During the following,* TIKO *might cover* PIGO *in tapa cloths.*

OTHERMOTHER. In the beginning there was only Ta'aroa, the being with no parents. For countless ages, Ta'aroa existed, floating in darkness in egg-like shells. Finally, wearying of solitude, Ta'aroa broke from the egg-like shells and, through thought, created a daughter – Hina, the moon, who has a face in front and a face behind. Then Ta'aroa lay with Hina, and they made Tane, Stratum Rock, Man. Then Ta'aroa bade Tane and Hina to cohabit as husband and wife… Or if you were to go two days by sea across to the Tuamotu Islands, then it was Tefatu and Hina who begat Ti'i… Or if you went a day further over the sea to the Marquesas, Ta'aroa caused the shadow of a breadfruit tree – one of Ta'aroa's manifestations – to pass over Hina, and the warrior-god Oro was born, who slept with his mother to cause to grow the common people of the earth. So, you see, it all depends on where you start from. Oh yes, you're a long, long way from Adam and Eve now. You cannot run any further than this. What your Adam and Eve gonna do, eh, with no Original Sin? That Original Sin of theirs, that was done a long, long way away from these islands. There ain't no heaven and hell here, there ain't no rewards in the hereafter. St Augustine? He would be a light snack, and his nine hundred books would keep the oven fire going for half a season. We got no Oedipus here, we got no Virgin Mary. We don't worship virgins here. The women can sleep with whoever they want and we all bring up the children. There is food on the trees. This, as any syphilitic sailor could tell you, is paradise.

It is now morning. Suddenly, PIGO *sits up and vomits over his chest. His vomit is green from the arsenic.*

PIGO *shivers. He stands up, suddenly cold and sober.*
OTHERMOTHER *is making her own bed in the space where* TIKO *put his mat. She takes things out of her bags and hums to herself. The tune she hums is a lullaby and it is picked up gently by* BEN *on the guitar. It should sound like the 'Kosma Theme' from Jean Renoir's* Partie de Campagne – *spooky and wailing.*

PIGO. ...Well, it seems I am condemned to life. Ah well, maybe I got the day wrong.

TIKO. That was some big rain. The Lord has spared your soul. Like Moses in his little basket.

PIGO. There is no justice, that's the trouble. Surely I've been wicked enough to die by now?

TIKO. Ah, but that good old God, He cares 'bout every little asshole on every one of his creatures.

TIKO *opens a window shutter, which lets in a blinding shaft of white light. Outside, dogs are barking, girls are laughing.*

OTHERMOTHER *brings out a bottle of scented water and splashes* PIGO *with it. She hands him a rag to wipe himself with.*

PIGO. Thank you, madam... It's getting light, look. The shadows in the corner over there have become purple simply because of the complementary tones closest to them... Everything is colour... Like music, not form, not realistic representations... You know, a colour is only what it is by virtue of what is up against it. Oh, the violent harmonies when you dare to put a red next to a green... a purple with a yellow... a green next to a red... Everything is colour... Everything is relative... A red beside a green...

Crows cawing, people shouting, dogs barking, girls laughing and, of course, OTHERMOTHER *wailing her lullaby.* TIKO *shouts something to someone below. He comes back into the room.*

TIKO (*shouting*). Yes! He's up here! Come up! (*Then, to* PIGO.) Policeman come to get you. He says he give you five minutes to get your things. Then you got to go and be arrested.

There is a knock on the door. TIKO *goes to answer it. Silhouetted in the doorway we can see a dodgy-looking gendarme – maybe only half a uniform, a sarong on the bottom half.* PIGO *manages to stand alone. He inhales deeply and stands, unsteadily at first.*

PIGO. I am more than ready. I have no things. I guess there are those who can commit suicide and those who can't. I must be one who can't. What a disgrace.

PIGO *walks up to the light at the front door and leaves, walking past the dodgy gendarme.* BEN, OTHERMOTHER *and* TIKO *sing the wailing lullaby. The music is picked up and amplified.*

Fade out.

The End.

Glossary of Polynesian words

Arii'oi	High priest caste
Ala Loto Alofa	Road of the Loving Heart
Calaboosa	Local jail
Chinch	Evil Spirit
Fa'afafine	Transexual male/white woman
Ia Orana	Hello
Kanaka	Islander
Kaupoi	Rich man
Lavalava	Clothes
Long Pig	White man to be eaten
Mana	Spirit/soul/dignity
Maruru	Thank you
Noa noa	Fragrance
No atou	I don't give a damn
Pupa	White man ('whitey')
Ta'ate vahine	Man woman (ladyboy)
Tapa	Cloth/wrap-around
Te Fa'aruru	I make you shake (fuck)
Tiapolo	Devil
Tupapa'o	Ghost/spirit of dead ancestor
Tusitala	Teller/writer of stories
Vahine	Island woman

A Nick Hern Book

Death of Long Pig first published in Great Britain as a paperback original in 2009 by Nick Hern Books Limited, 14 Larden Road, London W3 7ST, in association with the Finborough Theatre, London

Death of Long Pig copyright © 2009 Nigel Planer

Nigel Planer has asserted his right to be identified as the author of this work

Cover image: Liam Bowers and Chris Rixon
Cover design: Ned Hoste, 2H

Typeset by Nick Hern Books, London
Printed and bound in Great Britain by
CPI Antony Rowe, Chippenham, Wiltshire

A CIP catalogue record for this book is available from the British Library

ISBN 978 1 84842 041 0